FEDERICO FELLINI

COMMENTS ON FILM

Edited by

GIOVANNI GRAZZINI

Translation by

Joseph Henry

The Press

at

California State University, Fresno

Fresno, California 93740

Original title
Federico Fellini
Intervista sul Cinema

© GIUS. LATERZA & FIGLI Spa, Roma-Bari 1983

English Editor: Carla Jean Millar
Cover Design: George McCann
Technical Advisor: Randy Dotta-Dovidio
Production Supervisor: Rosie Gutierrez

TRANSLATOR'S NOTE

Like the images he creates, the simplest statements of Federico Fellini have their own complexity. For as he explains to us throughout this book, life for him is a constant interplay between reality and fantasy, between surface and the mystery that lies beneath. Fellini the schoolboy does his time in the classroom while his inner self roams the quays of Rimini and runs off to join the circus. Fellini the director records everyday images the while reshaping them to fit his dreams. Fellini the commentator disclaims knowledge of all worlds except that of the cinema, then goes on to analyze those other worlds with keen perception. Youth and age; religion and politics; psychology and symbolism; and Italy distilled, the reality become the dream—all these are filtered through the dual lens of his own especial vision.

If that were all this book contained it would be enough. But add to that the shards of bedrock pragmatism so typically European and the tongue in cheek touches so typically Fellini—heaviness and lightness unsettling the mixture even more—and the general result is a unique and remarkable foray. The specific result is a close-up view of the life and thought, the appearance and reality of one of the most gifted and challenging filmmakers of our time.

Appearance and reality even slope over into the translator's chore, for what seems to be a straightforward interview is really a great deal more. The content and sequence of the questions by film critic Giovanni Grazzini are masterful, designed to elicit responses of the utmost breadth and depth. From those the reader will learn the how and why of Fellini's view of film making, and to a great extent the how and why of the man himself—provided the reader can distinguish between reality and imagination, fact and fantasy.

Finally, and this is immediately obvious, Fellini's responses are hardly unstructured chit-chat. They are visual essays, subtly personal, as probing as a scalpel, and verbally striking—"doodle" and "kaboodle" cohabit with "parasangs" and "amniotic sacs" to suggest an eye directed toward the printed page. Too, the richness of conjecture and anecdote is another giveaway that these responses are essentially literature with the surface appearance of conversation. Thus not only must the translator transmute Ciceronian sentences aglow with dependent clauses into blunt subject-predicate Anglo Saxon; he must also follow Fellini in disguising a torrent of thought and crafted narrative with the translucent mask of easy conversation.

Let the reader beware.

J.H.

Grazzini

Fellini

You are over sixty years old. Does it disturb you to grow old?

Ah, yes, I am sixty-four years old. I repeat that often to convince myself of it, yet I keep listening with my inner ear to hear whether something has changed, something has rusted, broken: in sum, to hear what someone sixty-four years old feels and thinks. The first time I was in Rome I lived in a *pensione* and had as a neighbor a Roman worker some forty years old who tried very hard to appear younger. He was always at the barber, used poultices, wore little waxed masks. Sundays he would spend the whole day in bed and evenings went to sleep with two slices of raw meat, one on each cheek, held in place by elastic bands. In the morning I would often see him come out of his room in his dressing gown, close the door behind him, stand motionless for several moments with his hand on the door handle, then suddenly reopen the door and thrust his head in. My curiosity aroused, I asked him one morning why he did that.

At first he didn't seem to want to answer me, but then looking me straight in the eye he said that by quickly thrusting his head back into the room after having closed the door for a bit he could smell whether there was the stench of old age. He invited me to check it out, shutting the door slowly. "Sniff. Do you smell the stench of old age?"

For a while I thought of that character each time I left my bedroom, and a couple of times I even checked his theory by opening my door suddenly, right after leaving the room, and sniffing the air while my heart skipped a beat.

"Old age," says Simone de Beauvoir "seizes you all of a sudden." Absolutely true. Until recently I was always the youngest in any group, at any meeting, at any dinner party. How the devil could it happen that in the course of a few hours, a day, let's even say a week, I could suddenly become the oldest. Yet I don't seem to have changed a bit. A little more insomnia perhaps, some lapses of memory, a decline in ability so that around five in the afternoon I have to cancel the orgies and revels I'd planned that morning.

If in my work as director I had to present a sixty-four year old realistically I would advise the actor to walk stooped over a little, to cough every now and then, to squint, and to cup his ear with a trembling hand, the way script writer Ennio Flaiano and I did some thirty years ago when we used to have fun clowning around pretending to be very old and hospitalized. "Sister!" Flaiano would call out, shuffling his feet, "I made caca in my pants!" I used to play the part of an enraged German nun who would arrive with a bucket of water and a big brush and wash him the way you wash a sweaty elephant. Then there was our scene of the two little old men in the public park who ogled the young girls and slobbered with joy, all without ever remembering what one did with young girls. Pinelli, a future film director, who was there watching us, laughed, but only a little, being somewhat older than we.

But why have we begun with that question?

Interviews with politicians, writers, philosophers, scientists have already appeared in this series of books. You are its first film person. How do you feel being in that company?

A little afield. Incredulous, unconvinced, which may seem like pretending to false modesty, but isn't. I don't seem to have changed much from the time I was seventeen with an eager if reckless curiosity, always postponing till the next day a more serious and responsible outlook on life. Even now that feeling of waiting avidly for the sound of the last school bell of the day seems shamefully real

Juliet of the Spirits

to me. There were classes that I sometimes delighted in, but who knows what was happening in the Piazza at that moment, or down on the pier, or at the fish market, or along the river? I always imagined that in my absence fascinating extraordinary events, meetings, stories were taking place. . . Even now with you, dear Grazzini, I can't help thinking who knows what splendid woman is crossing the Piazza San Silvestro at this moment. Why don't we go and see instead of staying here and interviewing me? What's the point of this banal ritual of questions and answers?

Because they haven't yet invented a better way of looking into an artist's attic storeroom, and one never tires of rummaging through yours.
I see I'll be chatting in a freewheeling manner for half an hour after each of your questions. So what I'm about to tell you will seem contradictory: but in truth I never know the right thing to say because I'm never sure who and what you are interviewing. What I mean is that the most embarrassing and schizophrenic aspect of an interview is the fact that the person interviewed must accept being someone else, someone who knows everything, who has universal ideas, world vision, and who can speak his piece about existence, religion, politics, love, suspenders.

I don't have any universal ideas and I think I feel better not having them. Therefore I feel uneasy in an interview which requires me to express them. With the advancing years I seem to have less need to understand—I mean understand in the sense of rationalize—my connection with reality. That, at least, is my way. I don't hope to systematize the world. What little I have to say, when I want to say it, I try to convey in my films, which I greatly enjoy making. You'll see, I won't answer a lot of questions. And during others I'll hide behind commonplace little stories more or less made up by me. And when you'll have put this booklet together I'll want to review it, correct it, and try to prevent its publication. I'll cross out questions and answers and try to rewrite them. What's facing us is a miserable time, disillusioning, angry, litigious. Maybe we won't speak to one another afterwards. All right. Let's get on with it.

I count one hundred and twenty-nine ballpoint pens, twenty-one pencils, and eighteen felt pens on your table. That seems a little much to me.

At the beginning of each film I spend the greater part of my time at the desk, and all I do is doodle tits and asses. It is my method of tracking the film, of beginning to decipher it by means of these scrawls. It is a kind of Ariadne's thread for getting out of the labyrinth.

By the way, a book of your sketches has come out recently. Even more than a collection of handsome designs, it gives the impression of glancing through a "family album" of your films. It's like entering the attic storeroom of Fireater, from Pinocchio, *and setting all the puppets free.*

I don't know where all those doodles came from. I don't mean I don't recognize them. I made them. They are ones I sketched on sheets of large white paper during the preparation of my films. It's a kind of mania I have, always scribbling. Even when I was little I spent hours fooling around with pencils, crayons, chalk, on all the white surfaces at hand— sheets of paper, walls, napkins, restaurant tablecloths. Even the driver's license I have in my pocket is filled with little designs. But as regards the designs I sketched at the beginning of each film, they are a way of making notes, of fixing ideas. Some people get a quick handle on things by means of words, by sensations. I design. I sketch the traits of a face, the details of a costume, a person's attitudes, expressions, anatomy. That is my way of getting close to a film I'm making, of understanding what it is and beginning to look it in the eye. Later on these sketches, these shortened notes, end up in the hands of my collaborators. The scene designer, the costumer, the makeup man use them as models in preparing

7

Fellini: sketches for *Amarcord*

their work. That way they too begin to familiarize themselves with the mood of the story, with its nature, its connotations. Thus the film takes on a sense of anticipation, each sketch providing something to speculate about.

A German editor friend of mine told me he liked the sketches and wanted to make an album of them. And when he gave me the finished volume I must say that even I was intrigued. Besides the authority conferred on them by printing and by the innate dignity of any book, apart from the elegance of the groupings, the paging and the glossy paper, I was stupefied at seeing my designs all together. I considered them if not beautiful, at least intriguing, sincere little emblems mysteriously implying the style and intention of the film to which they belonged.

Laterza wants to go with yet another book of them, to round out that extemporaneous, haphazard anthology with a more organized, more documented project, better suited to the nature of his publishing house. And he has succeeded in tracking down my designs through friends, acquaintances, collaborators everywhere. A quantity of scribbles and sketches, caricatures, notations, jokes which I, who keep nothing, don't even remember having made.

Let's go on to a quick autobiographical sketch. Do you think you attained "success" as an artist by moving from cartoon humor to film writer? Is there a thread that ties your story together? Let's try to unravel it together, beginning on January 20, 1920 when you were born in Rimini under the sign of Capricorn. Do you place much belief in astrology?

I like to believe in everything that stimulates imagination and offers a more fascinating vision of the world and of life or, rather, one more congenial to my own way of living. Astrology is a very provocative system, and a fun way of interpreting the meaning of things, their how and why. And if someone feels safeguarded by that system, which does have its own rationale, what is the point of deluding him and telling him it is ridiculous fiction and that today it is no longer possible to believe in such nonsense.

It doesn't seem to me that things change much within us. We continue to have dreams identical to those which men had three or four thousand years ago, and in confronting life we have the same fears as always. I like being afraid; it is a sensuous feeling which gives a subtle pleasure. I have always been attracted by whatever makes me afraid. I think fear is a healthy feeling, indispensable to enjoying life. I consider it absurd and dangerous to rid oneself of fear. Lunatics are without fear, and supermen in comic books; also super heroes. In school I instinctively disliked Achilles. How could anyone be so inhuman, never afraid of anything? I don't mean I consult the horoscope in the weekly papers in order to know whom I'll meet in the afternoon or throw the *I Ching* coins in the air to decide which necktie to put on in the morning. To tell the truth, I feel more safeguarded by what I don't know about and am more at ease in uncertain, half-hidden, shadowy situations. I believe that because I am what I am the unusual, the unheard, the marvelous, or let's say more modestly the strange, often await me at some bend in the road. Therefore I have had my astrological phase, occultism, seances. And since we're discussing this, let me add that while I was preparing *Juliet of the Spirits* I knew and frequented mediums and sensitives endowed with such extraordinary powers as to stifle the snobbish, unshakable certainty of some of my friends who often snickered at my tendency to be excited by whatever reveals a subtler form of reality.

Besides, I can even testify to having been a party to unexplainable events. There was a time in my infancy when I suddenly saw relationships between colors and sounds. An ox mooing in my grandmother's barn? I beheld an enormous reddish-brown carpet floating in the air above me; it came nearer, backed away, became a narrow strip which

11

floated into my right ear. Three strokes of a bell? I saw three silver disks detach themselves from the bell, approach me while my eyebrows trembled, and disappear inside my head. I could go on like this for a good half hour. And how many "synchronous" experiences keep happening to me?!

It is Jung, if I'm not mistaken, who speaking of "synchronicity" refers not only to actions occurring at the same time but to more mysterious, inexplicable phenomena.

In trying to remember how Jung defines synchronicity, I think he means connections between outside events and inner states which in the light of logic should have no direct relationship. But because of their apparent diversity that relationship takes on profound importance. Perhaps I am not explaining myself well. I mean that Jung, in working out his idea, has tried to show us we can reach a more intimate understanding of the connections between the psychic and the material world. But most of us are so confused and defiant about whatever isn't controlled by the senses and by reason that those insights that come from deep within, those messages, warnings, bits of advice that not even the most intelligent and caring of our friends could give us, are completely ignored. We don't heed them, we become continually more deaf to them, more obtuse to the point of not receiving them any more.

It was on the basis of a synchronistic experience that I selected Freddie Jones for a major role in *The Ship Sails On.* I was full of doubts about him, studied him from all angles, face, three quarters view, and couldn't convince myself that this English actor with red hair, red skin, red all over, could become my Orlando, a droll, likeable Italian journalist. I had already checked hundreds of photographs of him, had made two long screen tests, and now while I was accompanying him by car to the airport and he was sleeping at my side with a beatified little smile on his lips, I looked at him with near hatred. "No, you cannot be my Orlando." I thought. And never was a face more alien and unknown to me. "Who are you anyhow?" I murmured with rage. And at that moment, as I was asking that question, above the window of a passing bus behind the profile of Freddie Jones, who was now snoring, a placard some twenty meters long filed past with the enormous printed word: "ORLANDO." I quit right there, all doubts canceled, and signed him up. Have you seen the film? He seemed perfect for the part. Perhaps Freddie Jones would be slightly resentful to know that I selected him not so much for his talent but because of the publicity a candy manufacturer was giving to ice cream cones called

"Orlando." Well, that's how it is. The ways of the Lord . . .

The same situation too with this interview: I had a warning which I hope doesn't involve synchronicity. Should I tell it to you? All right. Here I am in my study waiting to begin our chit-chat. What's the point, I ask myself, in going through the Nth interview when a little book has just come out with too much of this claptrap already? I am perplexed, unhappy. Wouldn't it be better to drop it? And while I'm having this thought my eye catches the newspaper I had left on the armchair: a headline six columns wide: "FATAL ERROR." That's what it said, leaving no room for misunderstanding. Or maybe there was room for misunderstanding, or better yet, for ambiguity, as in all oracular responses. Would the "fatal error" be doing the interview, or not doing it?

Do you feel very Roman?

I am half Roman, actually. My mother is Roman dating back many generations. A cousin of mine, interested in genealogy, discovered that the earliest information on the Barbiani (my mother's maiden name) appeared in 1400. There was a Barbiani associated with the pontifical court of Pope Martin V. He was an apothecary and was involved in a poisoning trial. He was thrown in jail where he

14

languished for some thirty years, training mice and spiders. Who knows? Maybe a little of my desire to be a movie director can be traced back to that remote ancestor.

Half Roman therefore, and in Rome indeed—when I came to settle here in 1938 I was soon more at ease than in my real home. What, though, is my Roman side? According to convention, Roman implies extroverted, sensual, generous, sociable; a lover of company, conversation, pleasant dinner tables; someone quite responsive to political frenzy; a blasphemer who proclaims himself an atheist but sends his wife and daughters to church because someone in the family has to maintain contact with that devil of an eternal Father. . . I don't think I'm a model for any of those likeable merits and defects. Especially as regards passion for politics, I am more Eskimo than Roman.

But how can you possibly not be interested in politics?
I am not a political person, have never been one. Politics and sports leave me completely cold, indifferent. I don't participate, and when I am traveling by train or a guest in someone's home my topics of conversation are therefore reduced to zero.

I'm not really bragging about this chronic indifference of mine to politics, which continuously makes me uneasy. Friends, present day society, and moral indignation should move me to adopt decisive, ideological positions and a more willing attitude to effect change, to overcome inertia. That machine balanced between good and evil, and within which I live and function, ought to run more smoothly, more functionally and with greater justice and greater dignity for all. But when that means a call to action, to practical activity, to joining groups, discussions, marches, declarations, confrontations, the very idea of being involved in that regulated world of debates and meetings drives me back into a neutral zone. I reject that Boy Scout activism, half a sense of duty, half something-to-do-after-work (always the basis of interest in "public affairs"). It is irresponsible, infantile perhaps; however I celebrate my escape from danger by occupying myself with the only thing that interests me, that is, making films. I recognize that mine may be a neurotic attitude, a refusal to grow up, conditioned in part perhaps by having been educated during Fascism and therefore excluded from any individual participation in politics except demonstrations and marches. From that time on I held the conviction that politics is the business of the "greats," performed by thoughtful gentlemen—as the history books tell us—for manifest destiny, for the fate of humanity. Those "greats" ought to have the slightly farcical manner of a Mussolini or the serious aspect of a Giolitti (as he appeared in the caricatures of Galantara). Or they ought to hark back to more seventeenth century, marmoreal models: Crispi, Rattazzi, Minghetti, Ricasoli the iron baronet, politicians always shown standing up in Parliament presenting a discourse to grave and bearded colleagues wearing black frock coats.

Perhaps the limits which constrain me today come from never having breathed, in my formative years, the true meaning of democracy outside of models as remote as science fiction. From my Greek lessons, from philosophy, I learned of the *polis*, government by the people, Athens, the citizen, rights and duties, Plato, Pericles, Socrates, the Socratic method. But democracy to live by, or to catch a glimpse of in American films, has not been an integral part of our culture. In American films the law is protected by the sheriff and all his volunteer deputies who get on their horses to chase the bad guys; or as it functions in the big cities with their skyscrapers, with people busy in their offices, with jobs, dignity, well being, freedom in which to boldly plan out a first rate existence. Or that Anglo-Saxon myth of democracy which their children breathe from six months on, learning to respect if not to share the decision of the majority, because they themselves have at hand the means

17

to become the majority and to change the course of history. All those lessons of civilization and of consciousness we perhaps lack, which has left us somehow with a conviction that politics should be practised by others, by those who know how to do it.

Even when things go differently and there is war, the collapse of a regime, a reconstruction period, and a new state that finally seems to align us with more civilized, more advanced, more important countries, democracy for us arrives as something intoxicating—a sudden freedom from the condition of individual subjection with which we lived for so long, for so many centuries. That condition has become a kind of biological state, a bodily function, a functional deformity difficult to remove or to ignore. Perhaps it's because I have lived in all this hodgepodge—see how confused I am in talking to you about it—I must confess, admitting my own limitations, that even now I have the feeling that other men ought to administer public affairs, make decisions, manage the everyday, the contingent, the ephemeral world where I find myself totally inexperienced and organically unfit. If we must accept particular destinies and certain tendencies, I do understand that an artist, and everyone who dedicates himself to expression, moves in totally different areas, those which are unchangeable or at least less subject to change or to violent revolution. Perhaps they are closer to conditions of the spirit, of wisdom, of the interior more than the external. In that oriental tale of *The Sorcerer's Apprentice* the book of knowledge that he arrives at after a long ascent is composed of pages made out of mirrors: which means, the only way of knowing is to know one's self. I don't know what value that can have to someone who every day must confront all the practical problems: mediations, balances, time constraints, depression, worry, the vote, the polls, the administration of society.

But why do you share the same basic dislike for sport as for politics?

I know that in a country like Italy I risk being lynched by saying I have never seen a soccer match, but it's a fact. I have never been interested in sports. When, for example, I happen to attend some match, basketball, water skiing, marathon, I am always bored. Sometimes as a child I used to retrieve balls at the tennis court of the Grand Hotel in Rimini. But it was a mystery to me how two men dressed in shorts could enjoy themselves batting a little ball from one side to the other hour after hour. One time I followed the Italian auto races as a reporter for the Ferrara newspaper

Corriere Padano, and all I could remember was deadly boredom, brutal fights, terrifying spills. After two reports I dropped it, or rather the director dropped me because I got the names wrong and I didn't use the necessary heroic, concerned, sympathetic writing style.

I might perhaps watch Graeco-Roman wrestling with a bit of interest, probably because I had a complex. Being thin as a skeleton I envied those young guys with all their muscles who could show off almost nude in front of everybody. But the competition, the struggle, the rivalry, the challenge left me bored or outright hostile. I definitely had a secret sympathy for the loser. And a situation that pitted one against another to determine who was stronger, more agile, braver, and therefore more beautiful, always provoked in me a feeling of isolation, of rejection, of rebellion.

The Thousand Mile race! That one I remember with pleasure. That was a main event, like Christmas, the birth of Rome, the Corso strewn with flowers, fireworks, all the dates that crown a year with extraordinary deeds, dates we look forward to, like fate. Too, the blessing of the animals in the church dedicated to St. Anthony of Padua was an exciting festival for me years ago. The braying, barking, cockadoodledooing, grunting, in the middle of which a brawny Friar would pretend that the chickens, turkeys, ducks and pigs were quiet during the function—otherwise he would not bless them. With his fist under the muzzle of a donkey he would snarl, "I'll give you a belt in the head instead of holy water!" (I'm digressing, I know, because I don't know what to say about sports.)

You were talking about the Thousand Mile...

Ah, yes... preparations for the route of the Thousand Mile would begin two days in advance. Out went all the stalls at the entrance and exit of the Corso. The shops were closed, and those with windows and balconies along the Corso were rented out for their weight in gold. The poorer people perched perilously on the roofs, and couriers on motorcycles and bikes were sent into the country as far as ten kilometers outside the city limits. Five or six hours before the race began there was no one in the streets; everyone was in doorways or at windows, like in boxes at the opera. The mayor, the count, the wife of the Fascist secretary watched through binoculars the Arch of Augustus at the end of the Corso where the first car would appear. Many people waved flags, others blankets; some gave the finger from windows to other windows across the street. There was no radio coverage then. No one knew who was winning the race. The only way we knew anything was from a phone call saying one hour ago they passed Parma. From that we could calculate that within fifty to seventy minutes the first car would come through the Corso. It was now all empty and cleaned except for the usual looney who, with delusions of grandeur, would come out peddling like a kangaroo and making noises with his mouth like the exhaust of a Bugatti. By twilight, as usual, a motorcyclist would announce with his trumpet that the first car was about to arrive. Bursts of shouting from all the windows: "It's Bordino! No, it's Campari! But it's Brilliperi, he recognized me, he nodded at me!" Then would come another idiot who, when a car appeared, would take off at high speed on his broken down petrol-bike desperately trying to stay alongside the roaring car for a few seconds. He held a casserole that he wanted to hand the racer at all costs. "Purée! my momma made it! It's good for you!" He would be arrested right away, and he and the police captain got to eat the purée in jail. Then the darkness would come. Cold supper at the windows, smooching, singing. That's the way it would go all night, with the terrifying roars and the flashes of cars suddenly swallowed up by darkness. At dawn, even the most eager were sleeping, their heads pressed against the window sill, opening tired eyes at the passage of the very last cars.

"Who was that?" The responses would become more and more obscene, and by seven in the morning it would all be over.

Did you do well in school?

From kindergarten through elementary school I don't remember anything. Ah, yes, in kindergarten the lay Sister from the Sisters of San Vincenzo, the ones who wore cloaks with sea gull wings: she had a shaven head, like convicts in humorous cartoons, and her face was always apoplectic red. I couldn't tell you the young girl's age, perhaps fifteen, twenty years old. What I remember is that she always embraced me, squeezed me, rubbed me against her body with its odor of potato skins, its stink of rancid soup and that smell that Sisters' cassocks have. Held like a little doll against that big, solid, warm body, one day I felt a giddiness, an early stirring, a tingling at the tip of my nose. I didn't know what it was, but it made me almost faint with pleasure. That was, I believe, my first violent sexual emotion, because even today the odor of potato skins makes me a little weak.

In elementary school my teacher Giovannini disappeared each Christmas and Easter behind a heaped up wall of gifts that we, like a conquered, servile people brought in, kneeling before his altar of food, smirking like pimps. We could hear his voice buried behind a wall of kilos of cheese, baskets full of chicken, cases of wines, ducks, turkeys. One time, Stacchiotti, a repeater who was still in the third grade at sixteen years of age, came to class with a live piglet, and that year he was promoted. I too remember passing from one class to another on the merits of the excellent parmesan cheese my father made me give the teacher before the holidays.

I have told about my high school days in *Amarcord*, and you can see from that film that I learned little in school. To compensate, I enjoyed myself a lot. More than Greek, Latin, mathematics, chemistry, none of which I remember any more— not a verse, a phrase, a digit, a formula—I learned to develop a spirit of observation. I learned to listen to the silence of passing time, to recognize far off sounds and odors coming through the windows opposite, somewhat like a prisoner who knows how long it takes for that little triangle of sun to reach his cot and to distinguish the bell of the Duomo from that of Sant'Agostino. I have pleasant, lazy memories of entire mornings and afternoons spent doing nothing, stretching my legs out under the bench, cleaning my nails with a pen point, thinking of Volpina, at that time surely at the seaside making love with the sailors behind the reefs. It was March: was she already stripped naked?

Then school for you was a "school of observation"...

Perhaps it was at school that I developed a certain humorous, caricaturist bent, a way of looking at people with irony and fellow feeling. Perhaps those teachers instilled it in me. They were really funny and pathetic despite their shouting, their eyes glittering behind their glasses, their insults, their tearing our homework apart as though it contained the most infamous heresies, their threats shouted in an unknown dialect: "You ought to be in jail, in a lunatic asylum, not in school!" Despite those neurotic, schizoid attitudes, or perhaps because of them, I felt great liking for them. They spoke with accents and dialects we had never heard before, except maybe in some jail-house from some *"giargianese"* cop. In Rimini *"giargianese"* means someone from the South. Matera, Reggio Calabria, Siracusa, Napoli were all *"giargianese"* to us. One of our schoolmates, from Ancona, we also called *"giargianese,"* which made him cry every time. In truth, when we spoke our own Rimini dialect we had the same chance of being understood by others as a Chinese speaking his own language with his head under water. But we would burst into impudent laughter when Professor De Nittis, reading Dante's Inferno to us, made the classroom resound with his cadences from Barletta.

Amarcord

Perhaps at school I also learned that there were many kinds of Italians and many little parts of Italy, each different from the others.

Since you mentioned Dante's Inferno, I would like to digress briefly and ask if it's true that you have been approached several times, by Americans particularly, to film The Divine Comedy. *The cinema has always been tempted by Dante's poem.*

Yes, it is true. That has been proposed to me on three or four occasions and always the faces of the interested parties lengthened with disappointment, unable to understand my reluctance. It was grave, very grave, unpardonable that I should say no to so lofty a project. The last time a large, absolutely likeable American, in an attempt to convince me, assured me that I alone could succeed in making Americans understand what Dante had gone to do in the Inferno.

The project is seductive. I would like to make about a half hour of lunatic, schizoid images—the Inferno as a psychotic dimension, reworking Signorelli, Giotto, Bosch, the sketches of lunatics: a tiny, stark, uncomfortable, tight, flat ambiguous Inferno. But generally the producer who proposes *The Divine Comedy* wants Gustave Doré: smoky scenery, beautiful naked asses and science fiction monsters.

A work of art is its own unique expression. Those transpositions from one art form to another I find monstrous, ridiculous, off the mark. My preferences are for original subjects written for the cinema. I believe the cinema doesn't need literature, needs only film writers, that is, people who express themselves according to the rhythms and the cadences intrinsic to film. Film is an autonomous art form which has no need of transpositions to a level which, in the best of cases, will always and forever be mere illustration. Each work of art thrives in the dimension which conceived it and through which it is expressed. What can one get from a book? Plot. But plot itself has no significance. It is the feeling which is expressed that matters, the imagination, atmosphere, illumination, in sum, the interpretation. Literary interpretation of events has nothing to do with cinematic interpretation of those same events. They are two completely different methods of expression.

Although you speak with sympathy and understanding about your schooling, it seems that you think it falls short of its obligation to educate children. If you were a minister of education how would you reform the school system?

I have no children. I have nephews whom I almost never see, and since I'm always busy making films I don't know what school is like today. I'd guess that apart from a certain revarnishing of the facade and a greater relaxing of discipline it is not very different from mine. That is, too little scope, and ill-equipped to take responsibility for student development. The child begins schooling at an age when the boundary between imagination and reality, between the opening world of knowledge and the ampler world of the irrational, of dream, of inner meaning is the thinnest of lines. It is still a porous membrane through which may flow the breath of change, infiltrating like osmosis. That state of grace disappears rapidly with the years. And far from being recognized and protected like a precious thing, a golden age of knowledge and capacity for living, it is totally ignored by the schools. It is eyed with suspicion, with dislike, an interference with the conventional order into which the child must be placed. This situation is no one's fault; it is part of the mental laziness, the list-lessness, the incompetence with which we generally address problems of education, persuaded as we are that the child is a total mistake which must be remedied. We are, however, dealing with a strange, unusual being who has the means, still rudimentary but intact, to put itself in touch with reality and who, like the natural elements, retains knowledge that we have lost. It knows so many things forgotten by us or forcefully blocked out.

If I had a son I would try first of all to learn from him. Parents normally do the opposite. They impose on their son the few bits of nonsense they know and don't ever ask him about anything. I have never seen a parent bend over to his child to ask what he is doing, what he wants, what the cat looks like to him, what of the rain, what he dreamed of in the night, or why he is afraid. We are totally taken up by our own problems, by our own myopic vision of reality.

I have always been attracted by this strange little being with his wry comic faces, by his tyranny, his ferocity, and his look of animal innocence. The film I most regret not having made—but it would be practically impossible—is a story about some thirty children, two to three years old, who live in a large house at the edge of a city. I am intrigued by the mysterious telepathic communication among infants, the glances they exchange when they meet on stairways or on landings, behind a door or in a cradle, or when they are held by the hand like bunches of vegetables. A film about life in an enormous house, all reflecting the viewpoint and imagination of children, with their stories of absolute love, hatreds, unhappiness, all told on stairways, on landings, in little fronting gardens— until those children, dragged out like hunted criminals, are brought to kindergarten and there, on the first day, castrated.

Of all my projects still undone, that one is the one which, along with *Mastorna*, continually reappears with an air of reproach. It could be a moving and infinitely comic film. Those children seem to me storehouses of great riches. They have a tiny, yet enormous, vault within their heads, their hearts, their bellies, containing secrets which bit by bit will disappear.

Let us return to your childhood memories. What kind of child were you?

Sometimes I happen upon old photographs where there I am in a sailor suit, standing alongside my brother, behind my father and mother seated on two velvet armchairs. I remember we had to carry them from home to the photographer's studio, a Socialist and under surveillance by the police. My mother insisted on being photographed in that armchair with her little dog Titina in her lap, named in honor of General Nobile who at that time was having his troubles on the Polar ice floes.

In another photograph I am plunked in the middle of forty school friends, and I play the buffoon, curved and hunchbacked like Lon Chaney in *The Hunchback of Notre Dame*. In another I am alone, very thin, with a red and blue bathing suit that comes down to my knees, smiling, eyes heavenward, like an innocent calf, my hair stuck

31

together with brilliantine and an unspeakable spit curl on my forehead; who knows what they had to promise me to get me to make that picture.

I study those photographs: can anyone comprehend what kind of child was there? Was he good? Was he sincere? Was he happy? And what has remained of that delicate, almost feminine baby? I have said on other occasions that although I am often described as the "director of memories" I remember very little of my childhood life. But to make you happy, here is my memory of an episode which, in the hands of a psychoanalyst could suggest character, vocation, and even a hint of destiny. I liked to be pitied, to appear unreadable, mysterious. I liked to be misunderstood, to feel myself a victim, unknowable. One time, seized by who knows what notion of revenge, I set the scene for a suicide. I rubbed my forehead and hands with red ink stolen from my father's office and stretched out on the ice cold pavement at the bottom of the stairway. There silently, without breathing, I set about waiting for someone to come by and let loose the first shriek of horror. My heart was beating strongly; the floor was so cold that I got a cramp in my calf which made my whole leg tremble. "So much the better," I thought, "to be shaking with agony." But I was also afraid that my mother seeing me this way would throw herself, crazed with grief, off the top of the stairs. "Let us hope not." I prayed, and held tight, waiting, deeply touched by my unhappy fate. Then someone opened the door and I felt myself tapped on the knee with the tip of a cane. It was my uncle, his face expressionless. From his height of over six feet he said, "Get up little buffoon, go wash your face!" I thought I would die for real, of rage, of embarrassment, and for years and years I hated that intelligent, heartless uncle.

When the Ethiopian war broke out you were in your first year of high school. What do you remember of it?
The departure of the volunteers from Rimini, amid flags and flasks of wine, with the people watching them dumbfounded. We saw faces wearing helmets and uniforms whom we could never imagine with a knapsack on their backs and a rifle with bayonet in their hands. There was Gigin of the Ditches, called that because he took care of all his bodily needs in a ditch behind the jail, to the rage and scandal of the washerwomen who threw wooden shoes at him and hunks of soap the size of bricks. Then there was Ciapalos, his nickname untranslatable and totally obscene. There was the son of the prefect, called "the lovely Wart"; there was Charlie Chaplin, who should have been a priest except that he fell in love with an ice cream

salesgirl; there was Rodriguez, middleweight champion, with a face that earned him the name of Sing-Sing; and then there came the toothless one, from the many blows he'd been given, singing *Little Blackfaced Girl.* And all the rest sang the chorus, casting ferocious glances around as if accusing all of us who stayed behind. With wild screams, then more songs and the waving of black and tricolor flags, the parade moved on amid a great cloud of dust. And from a window some eager soul, whether from joy or anger, threw an orange right in the face of the telegrapher who was patriotically waving a red white and green flag.

I remember posters hung on the walls of Rimini in which a legionnaire with an axe broke the chains binding an entire family of blacks. And the first postcards of the black women with naked breasts. And the technical analysis pronounced in a calm voice by Gigino Melandri, our great expert in exotic beauty. "You see, children, the Negress has small tits, set wide apart, and they can't be sucked together. But if you put your mouth in the middle you can lick, tick tock, right and left. The result for the subject is that one lick has equal value for both nipples." We listened to him in admiring silence and we all wanted to try it out, inviting friends to play the black lady.

I also remember the usual clowning around at school, when we went in groups of three or four to the principal and with voices trembling with emotional fervor asked the good man to give us the flag in order to celebrate our glorious soldiers who the evening before had triumphantly entered... "Where?" asked the principal a meek man, a former librarian, with a big pale nose which made him look like a rabbit. "Where did they enter?" And we, alertly: "At Waffankul, Mr. Principal, near Tolintesac." The poor man must have suspected the actual existence of those places, but he didn't have the nerve to object. Because once the Secretary of the Party, in a speech at the beginning of the school year, had said yes, Leopardi was good but take him with a grain of salt, because there is better poetry, namely patriotic poetry. And the principal, for whom Leopardi was God, felt as if he were under serious surveillance. So he gave us the flag and we, wickedly joyful, ran off to demonstrate under the windows of the scientific school, the technical school, and the law school, liberating all those other students. And we all went down to the sea to celebrate Waffankul.

How much truth is there in the story that you ran off to join a circus?

The truth is that I would have liked it very much to be true. I'm a little embarrassed to be still talking about the circus after having talked about it in all my films. I can say that relationships between reality and fantasy had already existed for me, more or less mysterious and inexplicable. It was a kind of exalting, prophetic reverberation that I felt the first time I set foot in the breathing, humid, silent big top. I was right at home in that great enchanted vault with its damp sawdust, its hammer blows, its deafening noises from everywhere, and the neighing of a horse. . . . It was the circus of Pierino which I have already told about in *Clowns*, probably a very little circus but it seemed immense to me, a spaceship, a hot air balloon, something I would have traveled with.

When show time came and the trumpets, the lights, the rolls of drums, the capers of the shouting clowns with their shambling, ridiculous, tattered, hilarious fooleries exploded all around me while I sat on my father's knee, it seemed in a fuzzy way that I was expected there, that they were waiting for me. They seemed to recognize me, like Fireater's puppets when they come out on the stage and see Pinocchio on a string and greet him as one of them, calling him by name, embracing him and dancing together all night long. In fact, I returned to the circus every day as long as it remained camped near the house, staying to watch the rehearsals and all the shows. One time the family searched desperately for me until midnight, and it

The Clowns

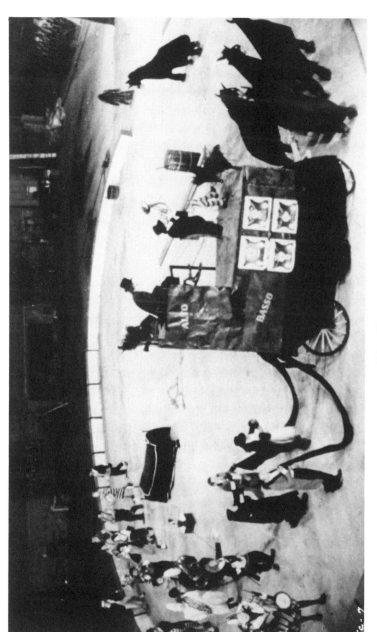

The Clowns

never occurred to any of them that I might be a few steps away from them. But my absence was reported elsewhere, and a week later Professor Rivo Giovannini gave me a public reprimand. "We have a clown in class." he said, pointing me out with his cane. And I almost fainted with pleasure.

Your adolescence, what did you do, what did you think?

What should a kid think who lived in the provinces with his family, with Fascism, the Church, school, American movies, and in the summer the German women in bathing suits on the beach. I don't have any spectacular memories, and besides I emptied them all into films I have made. By turning them over to the public I canceled them out. Now I can't distinguish what really happened from what I made up. Superimposed on my real memories are painted memories of a plastic sea, and characters from my adolescence in Rimini are elbowed aside by actors or extras who interpreted them in my films. I have emptied my storehouse of memories for that period; give me a little time and I'll invent new ones. The Americans have insisted on my making *Amarcord No. 2* for five or six years now.

Rimini...

A great flash of sun, summer, and in winter the fog which makes everything disappear. The fog is a great existential experience. Rimini in winter no longer exists. The Piazza is gone, the City Hall is gone, and the Temple of Malatesta, where has it ended up? The fog hides you from the others, gives you a more exciting hiding place, turns you into the invisible man. They don't see you and therefore you're not there. That fact thrilled me enough to make my flesh tingle. The most powerful memories of my adolescence are bound up in great part with natural events, always vividly scenic, which I loved to witness and sometimes to provoke.

I think I always had a certain tendency to interpret things through fantasy, a certain visionary quality. The disappearance of the Duomo, swallowed up by fog, moved me powerfully. In summer the great shadow of the Vittorio Emanuele Theater cutting across the Piazza Cavour was another enchanting spectacle. Or perhaps I wanted to feel enchanted in order to seem different from my school friends who didn't understand why I made such a big thing about the shadow dividing the Piazza in two. The instinct for spectacle always caught me up. I would use colors to disguise myself, from early childhood. One day an older cousin came from Bologna and I couldn't wait to steal her lipstick, lock myself in the bathroom and smear it on my face.

When did you begin to ask yourself questions?
I never did. I don't even do it today, and I don't understand why you are doing it to me. Since I don't know the answers I don't see why I should embarrass myself with questions. From my high school classes in philosophy I remember only the professor. His name was Dell'Amore and he came from Avellino. He wrote poetry like D'Annunzio, very sensual, and once a month he read it to us. His face was handsome and dark from the southern sun, his glasses gleamed; he had long hair (the kind you often see in police stations), holes in his socks, slightly pockmarked skin, and large moist lips over which he slowly ran a big red tongue. I liked him very much, but in class there was a certain Timbracci Duilio, son of an absolute bigot who in religious processions, dressed as a phantom, carried the cross and sang with a menacing scowl. (During one of these processions he had a slight attack, poor man, and collapsed, his large cross breaking a store front window.) It was his son who acted the spy for the principal, telling him that Professor Dell'Amore was reading dirty poetry in class during philosophy hour. From that time on, whenever we asked him to recite his poetry, Dell'Amore flattered

but regretful, said no. He begged us not to insist and would launch into a lecture on Spinoza.

Until that school year I never knew that there was a branch of knowledge which taught us who we are and where we are going. I listened to the opening philosophy lectures fascinated. It seemed to me that finally someone had arrived at our school who could tell us interesting things, besides Professor De Nittis who read Homer like the great tragedian Ermete Zacconi and moved us to tears.

I must add however that I remember very little of all those optimistic interpretations of human thought, all those universal concepts. School and life were two profoundly separate things. Very rarely did the school world, abstract, paper pushing, persecuting, shine light on humanity either concretely or by means of real imagination. Of all the lessons of likeable Professor Dell'Amore, I remember only his defiant and satisfied smile when, after silencing us, he asked in a near whisper: "According to you, dear children, if swift footed Achilles and a turtle raced one another, who would get there first?" Destroying his complacency I got up and said: "The turtle!" Naturally I couldn't explain why, but luckily for us Zeno had already resolved this baffling dilemma many centuries before.

On to Florence. Why to Florence exactly?

Because Nerbini's weekly humorous *420* was there, where I had sent vignettes and sketches. And because it was much closer to Rimini than Rome or Milan. I was still in high school when one morning I took the train and presented myself at the *420* editorial offices, where I knew the artist-designer Giove Toppi. He was the mainstay of all Nerbini publications, did the covers for *Buffalo Bill, The Three Boy Scouts, Lord Lister*, and the postcards for Little Blackface, the pretty black Ethiopian girl, as well as most of the vignettes for *420*. He also illustrated children's stories, posters. . . he belonged to the school of "figurine artists," as they called those disciples of Carlo Chiostri, the legendary illustrator of *Pinocchio*.

With his big nose, his white whiskers, a heating pad on his paunch, Giove Toppi stayed day and night behind the immense drawing table in a huge room that to me, coming from Rimini, seemed quite beautiful. It was like the *Vittoriale*, D'Annunzio's home: carpets, curtains, statues, shields, female nudes, armor, and way in the back a huge bed the size of a ship, all buried under pillows. Toppi greeted me as if it was quite normal for me to be there. He didn't look at me, continued sketching and meanwhile asked me if I knew in Rimini a dark skinned girl with green eyes who had beaten him at arm wrestling. I imagine he liked to play the role of someone who helps young people to take their first step. In the curve of his hand where he held his pen I saw the head of a little bird, and Giove Toppi, still without looking at me, explained: "He wants to be here, not in my left hand, just in the one with which I must sketch. If I let him go for even a moment he weeps desperately. You hear it? It touches my heart." He put the bird back into his warm right hand, sighed and began sketching again.

And that's how you were taken on by 420.

Yes, but almost a year later, because I had to finish school. When it came to applying to the university I came up against a blank wall, alone, uncertain. "All my companions were sure, I alone was confused." That is what Lao-tze said (pardon the quote, but I assure you it's the only one I will allow myself in the whole interview). I only knew what I wouldn't be: not a lawyer, which my father wanted, not a doctor, which my mother wanted, nor an engineer or an admiral. Writer? Painter? I was very interested in a career as special envoy for a newspaper and strongly attracted by comic actors, whom I consider the benefactors of humankind. To make people laugh has always seemed to me the most privileged of vocations, a little like that of a saint.

But surely you didn't only see comic films during those years.

Greta Garbo, Gary Cooper, Tom Mix didn't move me as much as Keaton, Laurel and Hardy. I couldn't stand Humphrey Bogart. I couldn't understand how someone could always be so angry that he even wore his trench coat to bed. Garbo inspired awe: lofty, abstract, constantly concerned with affairs of state, which seemed a little strange to us schoolboys. The Marx brothers blew my mind. They were my spiritual ancestors. I liked Buster Keaton more than Chaplin, who filled me with a certain distrust with his clear cat's eyes and his pointy rodent's teeth. I admit that perhaps he was greater, but Keaton doesn't trick you with sentimentality; his struggles, his disasters don't happen in order to right wrongs or injustices, don't try to move you or arouse indignation. His main strength is in suggesting a point of view, a completely different outlook, almost a philosophy, a different religion that overturns and ridicules all fixed and rigid formulas and ideas—a comic character directly out of Zen Buddhism. Indeed, Keaton has a stony faced oriental imperturbability. All of his humor is the humor of dreams where allegory, wit, and the comic aspect exist in the innermost depths, an enormous silent laughter at the immense irreconcilable contrast between our points of view and the mystery of things.

Let's return to Florence for a bit. Besides comic actors are there also writers whom you consider spiritual ancestors?

How I would like to find, once and for all, the courage to admit which books I have not read... what freedom, not to have to risk any more those chopped off phrases that prudently agree with someone else's judgment (but did he really read it?). Perhaps you're beginning to suspect how futile it is to continue interviewing someone like me. Very well, I will try to remember my spiritual ancestors: *Pinocchio, Bibi and Bobo*, Dickens, *Treasure Island*, Poe, *Archy and Mehitabel*, Jules Verne, Georges Simenon with whom I have become friends and whom I greatly admire (he told me he has made love to 10,000 women: could I ever become a writer like that?).

Then, in spite of school, I would like to add Homer, Catullus, Horace. I also like the *Anabasis* of Xenophon with those soldiers who each "forty parasangs ate olives and drank wine while leaning on their long spears." But how can we remember all the books that helped us grow up, revealing our selves to us? Do you remember Yambo? He wrote children's stories, illustrating them with sketches that seemed absolutely beautiful to me. He invented a character called Mestolino, who was a portrait of myself: a very skinny kid, hairy, constitutionally unable to tell the truth...

We were talking of your early experiences with editor Nerbini who published comic books. What did you do in Florence between 1937 and 1938?

I was something between an office boy and an editorial secretary. I stuck stamps on envelopes, and three or four times I carried the shopping bag for Aldo Palazzeschi from the market to his carriage. I didn't know he was a great writer then. What I saw was a kindly, quiet gentleman who liked to poke around the stalls, bargaining for salad, tomatoes, and cheese. The women in the marketplace called him Professor. One of them once called him Your Excellency and he laughed a lot at that. When I greeted him at his carriage he made me a half bow, calling me Your Excellency too, to the great amusement of his coachman, a sweaty muscular youth.

Another time Palazzeschi told me that at my age I shouldn't write those silly little stories for the journals but instead should write poetry. Many years later, reading *The Materassi Sisters* and especially *Roma* I had a feeling of embarrassment and shame because way back then I hadn't recognized the illuminating presence of a great master.

My friends then were Nerbini's writers and artists who put out *Buffalo Bill*, *The Three Boy Scouts*, *The Adventurer*, and *420*. When because of political tensions between Italy and America, American

American cartoons like *Flash Gordon, Mandrake the Magician* and others were barred from Italy, I boldly agreed, along with Gino Schiatti, to continue writing the texts while Giove Toppi illustrated them, imitating their drawings perfectly. After accurate researches, one commentator says that this story about homemade *Flash Gordon* cartoons is one of the many con jobs in my autobiography. Could be...

In December of 1938 you went to Rome to another comic journal, the Marc'Aurelio. *How did that happen?*
At school the *Marc'Aurelio* was a legend, one of those mysterious forbidden luxuries that came from afar, from a marvelous and dreamed about Rome, the way the films of Fred Astaire and Jean Harlow arrived from a hazy and remote America, that fabled, unattainable Atlantis. To get hold of the *Marc'Aurelio*, to read it, gave the same pleasure in forbidden things as there was in smoking secretly or trying to crash the casino by sticking close to the coat of an older friend. The little women of designer Barbara, the texts of Mosca, Metz, De Torres: those were legendary names and people. That most sought after biweekly didn't even make it to the kiosks. We had to go get it at the station when it arrived. We also had to overcome the constant opposition of the archpriest,

who once from the pulpit of the Duomo shouted: "Look what can be done with this dirty magazine instead of reading it!" Then came a moment of tension. What would he do with the magazine? To the disappointment of everyone he merely tore it into long thin strips and then rubbing them into balls with his hands he gave the impression of applauding himself.

One day at Riccione I recognized De Torres, his feet in the water, his red shorts pulled up to his stomach, and a newspaper on his head. It was he, I had no doubt! I had seen his caricature several times in the *Marc'Aurelio*. I didn't have the nerve to say a word to him, for he was lying there with his eyes closed enjoying the breeze, but I hovered around him all day long. Toward evening, seeing me still there, he asked me to get him a box of matches. Two days later I showed him designs, caricatures, little stories, and he told me to come to see him in Rome at the *Marc'Aurelio*. When I looked for him there a year later they told me that De Torres came there very rarely, that I would have to find him at the editorial offices of the *Piccolo*, a daily directed by Chief Executive Officer Baroni.

I'll bet Baroni was really something...
He wore a large hat bordered with silver, a camel's hair coat which came down to his shoes,

49

spats, a very long scarf and his shirtsleeves came out to the tips of his fingers. To us he seemed terribly elegant, and when toward ten in the evening we would hear his footsteps in the hall everybody got up to greet him. He would come slowly toward us in a cloud of cigarette smoke, the most beautiful women at his side, well known soubrettes from the theaters. Besides directing *Il Piccolo* he had another accomplishment: he could drop the smoky monocle which he wore in his left eye directly into the pocket of his vest with the precision of a juggler. An imperceptible movement of the eyebrow and click, the monocle disappeared into the pocket to the admiring comments of almost everyone. The only one who remained unmoved was writer Alberto Savinio, his beret on his head, his expression severe and aloof.

Editing the *Piccolo* wasn't at all like in the newspapers I had seen in those American films with Fred MacMurray or Joel McCrea, who tossed their hats from the doorway right onto the coatrack. One time Talarico tried it, but had to go down into the street to find his hat which had sailed through the window. From morning on, the halls of our editorial offices smelled of minestrone. I located De Torres in a little room with a table, chair and typewriter. He was all alone, enjoying the sun which came through the windows, eyes closed, smiling to himself, seeming content. I rapped, I coughed, I shuffled my feet. . . finally I decided to return later. By then the room was full of people, but of all the famous persons there the only one I recognized was Vitaliano Brancati, the Sicilian satiric novelist, because at school we had to memorize his account of his visit to Il Duce, and there was a photograph showing him alongside Mussolini.

Did De Torres commission your first article?
Yes, several days later, puffing with annoyance, he put me to the test. "Write a piece, let's see what you can do." he said pointing to the Remington on the table. And since it was raining he improvised in inspired tones: "I'll even give you the title: *Welcome Little Rainfall.* One page and four lines, no more, no less." And he went away satisfied, leaving me alone in front of that monster of a machine. I was very nervous. There was no Fred MacMurray and no humming of the printing presses from below. Still, it was a newspaper, and I was writing a piece, and in front of me was Ercole Patti turned toward the wall all hunched over the telephone whispering with his deep seductive voice, "Have you taken your drops?" I wrote the little piece, one page and four lines, in forty minutes.

Was it good? Was it published?

It was published many months later on the occasion of a light snowfall. Naturally the title was changed and also most of the article.

I didn't stay long at the *Piccolo*. Georges Simenon was my model and I looked to the scandal sheets as my chance to write articles that would capture a Maigret-like atmosphere. I interviewed concierges; I tried to go along in police vans when they made round ups of prostitutes; I was sure I was liked by the "bad guys." All I needed was one small incident, who knows, a suicide attempt with muriatic acid or someone jumping off a bridge so that I could write four or five pages in which I reported on the remarkable life and death of the victim, on his family, friends, acquaintances. Once, on the occasion of a suicide attempt (muriatic acid as usual) I went out to Colleferro where a former sweetheart of the would-be suicide had moved many years ago. She wasn't the beautiful woman I'd hoped to meet. On the contrary she was really ugly and ill-tempered, with a violent old father who at one point picked up a log and would have hit me on the head if I hadn't run away. I wrote it all up, but then I don't know who—the chief editor, the desk editor—cut my four pages down to six lines and added a headline that contradicted everything: "He drank muriatic acid mistaking it for water," or "Staggering on the parapet of the bridge he fell into the water." Betrayed, offended, even feeling a bit persecuted, I went off to the *Marc'Aurelio*. Right away I became editorial secretary. Vito de Bellis, the director, liked me and twice a week while we waited to go to the typographers, he invited me to dinner. With rough affection he taught me table manners: elbows at the sides, open your mouth only when the food is one millimeter from your lips, chew with your mouth closed, never look at your plate (frankly that rule seemed to me a bit obscure). And in the meantime he would tell about fabulous people: designer Galantara, the great actor Petrolini. Then we would go to typography in his car. I bought a pair of chamois gloves to handle the proofs, and I had a little table all my own with an architect's lamp. The typography was done in an enormous basement rumbling with the noise of the presses where I would stay until dawn. I was happy.

Did your cultural outlook change during that time?
One day a colleague, Marcello Marchesi, came from Milan with a book, *The Metamorphosis* by Franz Kafka. "Waking up one morning from a troubled dream, Gregor Samsa found himself transformed in his bed into an enormous insect." The

unconscious, which Dostoevsky had used to probe and analyze emotions became, in this book, material for the plot itself, the way fables used it, and myths, and darker more obscure legends. But the latter dealt with a collective unconscious, undifferentiated, metaphysical. Here was the individual unconscious, a shadow zone, a private cellar suddenly clarified by a glacial light, dismal and tragic, Jewish in its nature, akin to those great poet-prophets. Kafka moved me profoundly. I was struck by the way he confronted the mystery of things, their unknown quality, the sense of being in a labyrinth, and daily life turned magical.

I found quite a different outlook in American novels: Steinbeck, Faulkner, Saroyan. Finally life as it was, sensual, adventurous, pulsating. No parades, uniforms, collective rites, warlike victorious rhetoric. Instead a true feeling for people, for their daily struggle, their instincts. And an indefinable feeling of liberty, of streets without end traversing an enormous land, of lush countrysides without horizons but with a touch of something sacred and heroic, as in the films of John Ford. American literature and American films were a single unit—real life in glorious contrast to the gloomy life of high priests dressed in black who leapt through rings of fire: the individual winning over the collective. More than anything else the disappearance of American films and the sudden obliteration of any message from that culture gave us a real awareness of war.

We are now at 1941-43. Did you, in your twenties, have a glimmer of political conscience?

As long as the *Marc'Aurelio* was not suppressed or accused of stirring up revolt my answer must reflect the rude ignorance of a provincial student educated by the Church and by the Fascist regime. The only thoughts I had about liberty and revolt arose when a little column of mine in *Marc'Aurelio*, signed Federico, was forbidden. It consisted of letters from a girl to her fiance at the front lines. After the third article Minister Pavolini intervened. He met with me and director De Bellis and told us angrily that that young girl was a cry baby, fit only to demoralize brave soldiers at the front. No more column! Thus I bumped up against the stupidity, the absurdity of censorship for the first time. But for me it was a personal thing, not related to a more general or national situation.

During the editing of the *Marc'Aurelio*, however, every evening several editors, including Leo Longanesi (who would one day become the moving force of the great weekly, *Omnibus*) stayed late to discuss politics. Our editors often met with the *Omnibus* editors, who were also working at that time. That way I got to know Pannunzio, Benedetti, Flaiano, Landolfi and other future authors. They talked and talked and I, who remained there writing commentaries, listened in. I must confess, though without blushing, that what they talked about didn't seem to concern me directly. I couldn't understand what we ought to do. And even if I could have seen a need for conspiracy and revolt, how could we organize it? The faces of Longanesi, Ennio Flaiano, Marafini—who looked like Adolphe Menjou—were so good natured, kindly, comic, everyday, that they really couldn't convey the conventional image of conspirators. Perhaps they were, who knows? Flaiano never talked to me about it afterward during the films we wrote together.

Were you afraid during the war?

No. But not because I am particularly brave. Rather because I didn't know war in its atrocity, in its horror, in its insane killing. To better explain the coolness of this response, let me explain the conditioning of my generation. Ever since kindergarten war was so mythologized, so invoked. . . it seemed that the only way of life was war. For years and years we were indoctrinated by the Church and by Fascism into the myth of Romanness, the crucifix, Calvary, the worthlessness of life, the grandeur of heroism, sacrifice for one's country, mutilated unknown soldiers, a day of lions, *vivere non est necesse sed pugnare* [it is not necessary to live, only to fight] or something similar. . . it was a continuous bewildering delirious denial of life and its gentle, simple daily aspects. "Long live war!" "He who dies for his country has lived well." "Long live Sparta!"

How can one glimpse something different through that sinister fog? War seemed like a long-promised festival that was finally happening. I, however, did everything I could not to be invited, and I succeeded by bribing doctors and simulating mysterious illnesses. I spent three days in a sanitarium wearing undershorts and with a towel around my head like a maharajah. But when German doctors replaced Italian doctors, the series of convalescence permits they had given me for three years seemed inevitably at an end. A German doctor with drunkard's eyes gave me a packet of frightening papers and told me I had to rejoin *"unmittelbarunverzüglich"* ["immediately immediately"] my regiment in Greece (I understood that meant I had to hurry). But just as he finished saying "züglich" all hell broke loose. The Americans were bombing Bologna. Even the hospital I was in was hit, and there I was, all covered with plaster dust, running like a horse, minus one shoe, along hallways filled with people who were screaming, crying, falling to their knees while ambulance sirens howled and the earth shuddered and shook. From that day on I never heard any more about my military dossier. Perhaps it's better not to take this down, though. You never can tell. I wouldn't want some general to take it into his head to turn me into an infantryman.

In 1943 you married Giulietta Masina and in '44 you worked on Rome: Open City. *How did you come to work on that scenario?*

It was the scenario that came to work on me. I thought the cinema was finished. Italy had been liberated and everything was in the hands of the Americans, newspapers, radios, reviews. And on the screen there was only their films, to the great joy of a public that had never forgotten the stars of the one true cinema, the one that had brought them entertainment, dreams, escape, adventure. Who did we have? Besozzi, Viarisio, Macario, Greta Gonda (whom I liked very much; I also liked Leda Glori very much). How could they compete with the return of Gary Cooper, Clark Gable, the Marx brothers, Charlie Chaplin, and all those beautiful female stars and their script writers and directors? I was certain that our cinema would never be heard from again. Finished. Finished, the magic moment

Giulietta Masina in *Variety Lights*

of advance payment for signing a contract for a script, and that other marvelous moment, though a little less certain, of the second installment agreed upon. At times like the latter it was difficult to keep calm, to seem indifferent while the producer took out his plush leather bankbook where the checks were already there, made out in your name. Script writer Mangione, with whom I've worked, couldn't control his emotions at a time like this. His eyes shone and he pressed the check flat between his hands for fear it would lose its value if crumpled.

I thought that those times would never return again. I had opened the famous "Funny Face Shop" with some old friends from the *Marc'Aurelio*: caricatures, portraits, "very similar profiles," "records with your voices." I was artistic director for the shop, and the financier and administrator was my friend Forges Davanzati, an extremely fat young man who looked like King Farouk. He had a face as white as a jordan almond and elegant little waxed mustaches. He wore silk scarves and a pearl grey felt hat. The G.I.s who came into the shop liked him: perhaps they took him for an actor, the type who in American films plays the wicked fatty plopped in a bathtub in the middle of the jungle who makes the natives wash his back. I have to admit that I never earned as much per hour as at that time. The place had the atmosphere of a Western movie, something between a saloon and the waiting room of a brothel. We had some beautiful salesgirls who spoke three languages, and often the shop boy had to run across the street and make panic signs to the military police stationed right opposite our shop. All their jeep had to do was to make a U-turn with the siren mewling on low. Then in they would come, enormous, lithe and easy, four or five brutes, and without knowing who was right or wrong, without asking what was happening they began to club everyone in sight. My friends and I would manage to find protection under the tables, but Forges Davanzati, who owed a great deal of his reputation to his immobility, often took some terrible whacks across his stylish headgear, perhaps because he resembled that wicked fatty who whipped the black bearers.

Our G.I. models were tough, generous, and almost always drunk, but with a sense of humor that made us feel good. Seeing themselves caricatured would make them laugh for a whole half hour. They would stop in the middle of the street, doubled up with laughter. But before leaving they would leave on the table, besides payment in occupation lire of always double our fee, corned beef, beans and vegetables, cans of beer, and those brightly colored packs of American cigarettes, plastic and soft to the touch like a woman's arm. Had we been able to feel those packs before the war, anyone could have realized we would never win.

It was in the middle of such an uproar that director Rossellini came to find you one day.

Extremely pale, with a pointed chin and soft floppy hat, he was easy, quiet, cool and pensive. Maybe he was thinking it might be better for him to become my partner in the shop rather than stick to the proposal that had brought him to me: to invite me to write a scenario with Sergio Amidei, a tragicomedy on the life of Don Morosini, the embryo of *Rome: Open City*. But I have already told about these things too often...

That brings out an interesting aspect of your character: fear of repeating yourself. You presume to think that everybody already knows everything about you—or perhaps you're being lazy. At least, tell us how you worked with Tullio Pinelli.

It was like going to the office from morning to night. In the morning I went to his house and we scripted the more important films; in the afternoon he came to my house and in the evening, each in his own house, we worked for less important directors: Matarazzo, Righelli, Franciolini. Some of those directors were not really second rate. Gennaro Righelli was a most intelligent man, a charming storyteller. With his eye enlarged by a monocle and his beautiful Neapolitan voice he would speak of Matilde Serao and of poet Salvatore Di Giacomo, making a fabled Naples live again, like Baghdad or like Vienna under Franz Joseph. Pinelli and I would listen to him enchanted, our portable typewriters on our knees. And afterward to reward us "Commander" Gennaro Righelli would take off his elegant velvet jacket, tie on an apron, and go into the kitchen of his apartment in the Hotel Milan announcing it was time to prepare spaghetti with sauce supreme. One day producer Colamonici entered suddenly and caught us with three forks in midair. He howled like an animal, said that for five months he'd been paying the hotel bill and hadn't yet read a single line. Fortunately he became ill...

It was wonderful being a script writer. I had actually no responsibility because whatever I did was reworked by others, then by others still, and if there were anything good in the film I could always say it was mine. There were eight of us scripting *Document Z3*. We met in the beautiful home of producer Alfredo Guarini where all we did was drink whiskey, eat ice cream and smoke a lot. Sometimes Isa Miranda, the mistress of the house, would appear in that fog of smoke with a cake. Up we would all get shouting, "Here, here, signora! We'll take it!" Guarini would watch us affectionately, fraternally, with his soulful eyes and coming over to an armchair where a famous dramatist was sleeping he would caress his head delicately and ask us to make less noise...

How did you change from script writer to director?
I was working for Rossellini while he was turning out *Paisan*. Roberto and I had become friends. After the triumph of *Rome: Open City* in America and worldwide, he asked Sergio Amidei and me to collaborate on the script of his new film. Watching him at work I discovered for the first time, suddenly and clearly, that one could make a film with the same personal, direct intimacy with which a writer writes or a painter paints. That machine on his back, that Babel of voices, calls, movements, cranes, projectors, special effects, props, megaphones had seemed to me so threatening, so overwhelming and abusive when I was called into some studio to help write a scene or rewrite a dialogue. Rossellini discounted all of that, canceled it, relegated it to a noisy but useful corner in the neutral zone where the film artist composes his images the way a designer makes his designs on blank paper. He transformed that complex

interrelation, somewhat like an army on maneuvers, into direct contact with creative expression, something that had always before been hidden from me as if veiled.

For *Paisan* we were spared the indescribable confusion of a studio, since the film all took place outdoors in the real world. But there the chaos was even greater in those streets, in those cities, in the reality through which we moved. And it was remarkable to watch Rossellini stand still on the first floor shouting into a megaphone at a black actor while armored cars rolled on behind us and thousands of Neapolitans screamed from the windows, bargaining, sobbing, howling at one another.

If filmmaking was like that, if it could be done in that off-hand street-smart manner, and if it could be experienced as a continuous happening between life and a portrayal of life, then filmmaking seemed more the real me than script writing or scene design. And in filmmaking I would have to confront the same struggles, vexations, trials and errors as I did to achieve the script writing ideas I had in my head.

Wasn't that how I saw Rossellini work? Instinctively, without preconceptions, restricted very little by theoretical rules or rigid, empty conventions. It was his own style he was following,

the precision of his own expression. Just think of
the stupendous finale of *Paisan*, with the Germans
on the marshes of the Po dumping the partisans
into the water. Martelli, the projectionist, tore his
hair: "Can't be done, there's no more light." And
Rossellini who absolutely had to get back to Rome
for who knows which of his preoccupations—
perhaps a certificate of deposit had matured or he
had an appointment with some old maid—swearing
and cursing gave birth to a remarkable idea. With
only two cameras and with no scenic detail he shot
the scene long distance, and the sequence took on
an irresistible strength. You don't see the partisans
fall; you only hear them dropping into the water
one after the other. Did he hit upon that finale
because he had to finish and get away and run to
Rome, or was it the opposite? Had he created the
indispensable condition, the state of friction in
which the spark caught fire and dissolved the fog
that had held the idea prisoner? Was his exact
expression of that idea its clearest, most powerful
interpretation, perhaps its only true statement
among innumerable possibilities?

One might say—and some critics have not failed
to observe—that Roberto tended to extremes,
triggering off those mysterious effects too
mechanically, too obviously. However I think it was
from him that I finally learned the ability to maintain

a balance and to transform contrasts and adverse conditions into moving events, into feeling, into a point of view.

But Paisan *was not well understood when it came out.*

I remember extremely negative indignant criticisms, some of them abominable. In one newspaper I read: "The cloudy brain of the director doesn't clear up even for a moment in any of the six long episodes." It is a majestic film, extremely beautiful, as solemn as a Gregorian chant, rugged and moving. I saw it again some time ago and it brought back the same emotions that I felt so many years ago in Naples, when in the silence and the darkness of a little room I found Rossellini working at the Movieola. He was pale, his hair was tangled, and he stared fixedly at the little screen where he ran off a preliminary editing of the episode of the *Friars.* The images were silent; we heard only the rustling of the reels. I stayed there watching, enchanted, and what I saw seemed to me to have that buoyancy, that mystery and grace and simplicity that the cinema has been able to unite all together on only the rarest occasions.

You spoke of Paisan *and Rossellini with a moving enthusiasm. I gather that those were crucial months in your development.*

Traveling around filming *Paisan* became for me the discovery of Italy. Until then I had not seen much of it: Florence, Rome, and some brief tours in the South when I was going around showing films: tiny towns locked in a Medieval night, like those I had known as a child near Rimini on the Emilian Apennines. Only the dialect changed. Now, along with this moving discovery of my country I realized that the cinema offered this miraculous double feature: you tell a story and while you are doing so you are living another one yourself, an adventurous one with people as extraordinary as those in the film you are making. At times they are even more fascinating, worth portraying in another film in a spiral of invention-and-life, observation and creativity, spectator and actor, puppet master and marionette, special envoy and special event all at the same time, like people in the circus who live where they perform as well as on the trains in which they travel.

Paisan was a fundamental adventure in my life. It was beautiful to complete an episode, pack up, go off in the trucks and search for new locales. One day we wandered from morning till night along the muddy delta of the Po in search of a summer house called Baracca Pancirli that Rossellini remembered having seen when he was little, thirty, thirty-five years ago. We took as a guide a local who had a black patch over one eye. He told us that one night while stealing eels on the property of a countess she shot buckshot at him from the window. This squint-eye, who also limped a little, dragged us through mud and water all day without finding the summer house. At twilight he fell on his knees in front of Rossellini, inviting him to shoot him in the other eye. But we didn't have any guns. Then Rossellini began to laugh. Now he became the one who stubbornly kept us going, dragging the whole troupe behind him through a countryside out of a film by Kurosawa, with our trucks every now and then sinking down into the mud while great black birds flew lower and lower. Things began getting tense and the porters wanted to turn back. Rossellini jumped up on a jeep and made a speech, promising everybody a pint of rum. Night fell, and we didn't know where we were any more or even what we were doing in this constricting marsh. Suddenly a little child about three years old burst out of the reeds, who after having said in Venetian dialect, "I am a thothialitht," guided us rapidly to the Pancirli summer house which was a few steps away, quite close to the place where we had left from that morning.

We ate eels, dressed live and cooked on a brushwood fire. Night fell, like in the *Anabasis* of Xenophon.

I know that you don't go to the movies very often. Nevertheless who are the directors on the international scene—or the films—that most stimulate your interest?

With the passing years I have lost the habit of going to the movies. I can't explain this change convincingly even to myself except that even as a child I did not frequent movie houses often. I enjoyed standing in front of film posters and the huge photographs in the shops on the Corso announcing the coming programs. Maybe I liked to imagine the fascinating ritual taking place in the movie house more than watching the film. The movie house in Rimini was called Fulgor. I have already told about it in almost all my films. There is a large photograph of me in the lobby now, right above the box office, and I can't help thinking that when a film plays that they don't like, the people leaving will hold it against me sort of, and eye me with disappointment. Many years ago the owner of the movie house would stand near the box office, a man convinced he was Ronald Colman's double. To tell the truth he didn't look much like him, maybe a little bit when he stood in three-quarters profile with his hat shading one eye. But only if he stood still and held a cigarette between his fingers, a little to the right of his chin so that the smoke rose straight as a string along his face. He knew it, and he stood that way almost without breathing, motionless, between the entrance and the box office. There, behind the window, his wife tore off tickets and breast fed her fat baby, covering her bosom with a flowered shawl behind which one could hear sucking sounds and, from time to time, the shrieks of a toucan.

The owner would go to Bologna to preview the films shown in his movie house, and when he returned he always sounded mysterious. "Ah, I won't talk," he used to say, but with a great wagging of his head and a crescendo of curse words in dialect he made it clear that in Bologna he had witnessed extraordinary happenings. "Did he die?" we asked on pins and needles. "Die, my ass!" he snickered, losing some of Ronald Colman's aplomb. We looked at him admiring, full of envy. "And when is Jean Harlow coming?" "She'll be here at Christmas." He would announce with great certainty. "And Wallace Beery?" "At the end of January perhaps. But I don't know if I'll bring him."

One Sunday morning, standing behind a curtain, I saw him seated all alone in the orchestra, almost in darkness, staring at the blank screen and smoking silently.

Then there was the pharmacist's wife who came to the Fulgor to get felt up. She would see the film three or four times in a row while all around her a great circle of youths, including us, embarked on

the great adventure, changing seats continuously
in a slow advance nearer and nearer. She didn't look
at anyone, smoked slowly through the veil of her
hat, her moist lips outthrust, her half closed eyes
fixed on the screen while we, breathing hard and
with hearts near to bursting, made a big thing of
touching her thighs.

Then there was Baghino, who would stand in the
darkness behind the curtains in order to spy out
the slightest expression of annoyance on the faces
of the audience when Il Duce appeared on the
screen in the news. Then he would run to report
to the Fascists. One time a group of four wrapped
him up in a curtain and trussing him up like a
sausage hung him from the ceiling by his ankles
and head. He screamed like a wild beast up there,
but no one had the nerve to go and free him.

I should like to make a film about the Fulgor
movie house, narrating everything that happened
there. A whole generation was conditioned, and in
part protected, during the Fascist years by those
glowing shadows that told fascinating tales of a
richer, freer, happier and more enjoyable
country: America.

The first films I saw were at the Fulgor movie
house. The very first? I can remember it exactly,
because its images impressed me so profoundly that
I have tried to recreate them in all my films. It was

Amarcord

called *Maciste in Hell*. I saw it in my father's arms
while he stood among a great crowd of people, their
coats soaking wet because it was raining outside.
I remember a large woman with a naked belly, her
navel showing, and with darkened flashing eyes.
With an imperious gesture of her arm she made
a circle of fire spring up around Maciste, who was
also half naked.

Then there was Greta Garbo, white and funereal
with eyelashes like fans, and every time she closed
her eyes my mother would murmur: "What fine
acting!" Tom Mix, Rin Tin Tin, Charlie Chaplin
who made us weep in certain films, notwithstanding
those sharp rodent teeth which made him not
entirely likeable. On the other hand the big fat man
with the mustache and beard who chased him
hobbling on a plaster cast was wholly likeable. Our
chemistry teacher at school looked exactly like the
big man, and whenever a new Charlie Chaplin film
was on at the Fulgor there was a holiday in class
the next day. We would impudently ask the teacher
to do the faces that the big guy made when he got
a rap on the head and when, even funnier, a whack
on the fingers. The professor, more pleased than
annoyed, would wag his sausage-like eyebrows
rapidly and blow on his fingers which the boy next
to me, who imitated Chaplin beautifully, had hit.
We applauded with enthusiasm, throwing our

dictionaries in the air until one day we saw him come to class looking as though nothing had happened, but naked without his beard or mustaches; even his eyebrows had been considerably thinned out. It seems the principal was worried about the prestige of the institution and gave him some iron-clad conditions: off with the beard and mustaches right away, or off with the teacher.

You are digressing and haven't answered my question. Which films have impressed you most?

I must shamefully confess that I have never seen the film classics, never seen Murnau, Dreyer, Eisentein, not even later when I went to live in Rome and perhaps went more often to the movies—but only if a live show preceded them. I saw many films that way, seated behind the screen on a trunk along with some little ballerina muffled up in her wrap, who with her nose in the air, holding a cappuccino or her little husband's hand, followed, deeply moved, the pathetic vicissitudes of *The Voice in the Tempest*. Getting back to your question, I am tempted to answer that many film creators have stirred my emotions and regaled me with wonders, making me believe everything they were saying. The fabulous Kurosawa, ritual and magic like a spellbinding ceremony: we were supposed to make a film together in episodes, along with Bergman. Kurosawa wrote me a beautiful letter from Japan, full of bows and studied courtesies, but we didn't do the film. Bergman seems like an older brother to me, more serious, more unhappy perhaps, or perhaps less since his unhappiness seems frozen in an unresolvable contest with his fantasies—who knows which will win in the end. Meantime there are his films, which clearly dominate the match.

I like the Marx brothers, who write their own films, and Laurel and Hardy, two clowns full of innocence. I have always been struck by Buster Keaton's detached, impartial view of people, life, things, not at all like Charlie Chaplin, sentimental, romantic, shot through with the trappings of social criticism.

The film work of John Ford is a state of purity, sparse, unselfconscious. I like his strength, his disarming simplicity devoid of obscure, sterile sociological commentary. He is someone who loves film, who has lived for film, and who has made film a fable accessible to all, a fable most of all about life itself. Naturally I cite Rossellini: his free and easy approach to reality, always alert, clear, fervent; his ability to locate himself between precise and hazy places, between objective detachment and awkward involvement. Those things permit him to capture reality in all its aspects, to look at things inside and out simultaneously, to photograph the aura of things, to reveal what in life is ungraspable, baffling, magic. I like Kubrick, Orson Welles, Huston, Losey, Truffaut—I wouldn't want to forget anyone—Visconti, Hitchcock, Rosi, Lean...I admire Antonioni's severe and chaste rapport with film, like a monk-scientist. And to be honest to the end, I must add that certain 007 films also delight me a great deal. Behind their enameled surface and their glittering chain of adventures I hear the alarming rustle of a world of beetles, terrible, agonizing—our own world, fascinating and tremendous. Those films often manage to capture within a gloriously conventional form a piecemeal distorted crazy message about modern man. Then there is Buñuel; I have only seen one of his films and was enthusiastic about it. It made me want to go and see them all. It was *The Discreet Charm of the Bourgeoisie*. What a great and charming film!

You have spoken long and often about your films, and I don't want to make you repeat things already said. But in this case I also want to point out something. You have often said you never see your films again. What connection do you still have with them? How do you view this "family" of films today?

I seem to have always turned out the same film. It deals with images and deals only with those images using the same materials: perhaps from time to time from different points of view.

The connection I have with my films is in proportion to how the film develops and approaches its completion, a connection that is the same in all my films. One fine day the film on which I am working seems finished, sometimes even before the final retakes. In the studios that were mine come other troupes of actors setting up other sets. I view those presences as an intrusion, a violation, a sacrilege; they are "spoilers." Thus the end of my work seems like a dispersion, an undoing. Meanwhile something comes along that seems like starting again from the beginning: the editing phase. Now the connection becomes private, personal; no more confusion, no more outsiders, visitors, friends who one way or another constitute a healthful mixture during the shooting. I have to remain alone with my film and edit it. Then comes the first viewing in the projection room: "it" appears on the screen reduced by the Movieola where it still has fairly pleasant connotations for me as it comes on the screen in proper form. But it has already achieved autonomy. Its images belong to it; those which it captured plus those which I instilled. Is it still my film? Do I still recognize it? It now looks midway between a brother and a blackmailer. An umbilical cord still binds us, waiting for me to cut it. At this juncture I begin to withdraw from it, to avoid it, to dislike looking it straight in the eye. The mixture I wanted to extract from it is now decanted, and from then on my interest rapidly declines. I finish it, certainly I finish it, with increasing fussiness so as to back away from it more and more, and without the earlier friendship or the hard-won solidarity.

When the film is quite finished I abandon it with distaste. I have never seen one of my films in a public hall. I am assailed by a kind of prudery, sort of like someone who doesn't want to see a friend do things which he wouldn't do.

When I say I never see my films again, never review them, even friends smile and don't believe me. But such is the case. Maybe it's because my films aren't hither or yon; they are with me; they are me, and I don't need annual verifications or check-ups. To confront them on the screen or on television sets off a kind of alarm in me, like walking down the street and seeing a face looking at you in a window or a mirror and recognizing with dismay that it's you.

Very well, but you haven't answered my question. Since you strongly resist talking about your films individually, let me propose a kind of game: I name a title and you, like in free association tests, tell what comes into your mind. Let's begin: Variety Lights [co-directed with Alberto Lattuada].

The livid dawn. Waiting for "the livid dawn." And Peppino de Filippo in the stable of the large farm where we were gathered, talking to us about the Naples of his infancy: the San Carlino Theater, Antonio Petito the mythical clown named Totonno the fool, a whole picaresque world of glories and tatters, of adventures à la Till Eulenspiegel, Pinocchio, Don Quixote. Fabulous stories about delightful actors who we don't find any more, one of a kind. We used to listen enchanted while that stupendous clown entertained even himself with his stories, snickering maliciously at those lazy, arrogant characters until someone in production would rush in shouting, "The livid dawn! Here it is! Everybody out! It's the livid dawn!"

Thus it became a part of the scene design—"livid dawn"—and everybody, even the crudest among us, adopted that somewhat literary expression. Day after day, shaking their heads with exaggerated worry, they would say to Lattuada and me: "You see, nothing more to do this morning. We need that blessed livid dawn. Last month was full of livid dawns!" The livid dawn had become a "thing," like a basket, like railroad tracks, like something tangible to feel and taste. These in essence are the stories I prefer to remember about films, even the

Variety Lights

only things I remember: an unexpected storm, the countryside turned stormy so that we seek the best shelter we can find—under a tree, in the electrician's truck, the more crafty into a farmhouse somewhat like a military invasion, benevolently arrogant, ordering the farmers to prepare an omelet.

This nonchalance, this heedlessness, or more sympathetically, this games-playing, is part of the alienation of our profession. It makes us regard people and things as if the whole world was a set at our disposal, an immense prop department on which we lay our hands without asking permission. It is somewhat like a painter for whom objects, faces, houses, the sky are merely forms at his disposal. For the cinema everything becomes a still life without limits; even the feelings of others are something placed at our disposal. It is a delirium, a semi-divine intoxication from power. And this feeling which binds together adventurers, invaders, predators, wastrels, creates close ties, definitive friendships, at least as long as the magic knot which is the work on the film ties us all together. But when the last reflector light is barely dimmed and the journey ended, then the friendly affectionate feeling cools rapidly, and detachment and indifference return. We hardly recognize one another any more—until the next film when we find ourselves all together again, hugging one another with enthusiastic shouts and floods of memories.

What can you tell me about The White Sheik, *the first film you directed solo?*

Often in later years while preparing complex and difficult productions like *Satyricon, Roma, Casanova*, I have thought with nostalgia of *The White Sheik*. I would like to make it again, with the experience and detachment of now and the intention of playing with the story and characters more casually. As I have said many times, I didn't think I would become a director. Even after *Variety Lights*, which was a lukewarm success, I was certain I'd be staying in the limbo of script writing for who knows how much longer. Script writing seemed more my thing because of its collective irresponsibility, its lack of true commitment, its behind the bushes atmosphere with no obligations at all.

My first day of shooting was a total disaster. I didn't turn out a single frame. There is nothing more hopeless and difficult than to have a camera set on a raft in the open sea and trying to hold it still to frame a boatload of actors. The sea is like an immense back continuously moving. It takes just a second, re-checking the camera, to find nothing in the frame except the horizon or the blinding sun.

That morning (my first morning as director) I left the house at dawn, after having kissed Giulietta with feeling and having received rather skeptical good wishes from the housekeeper, who kept repeating from the doorway: "But you'll die of the

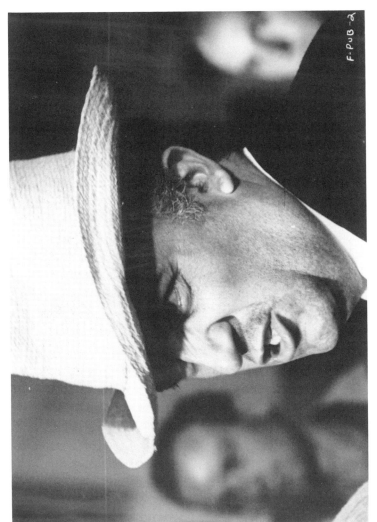

Fellini as Director

Fellini as Director

heat that way!" Although it was already summer I had dressed up like a director: shirt, boots, leggins, sunglasses and a whistle hanging from my neck like a soccer referee.

Rome was deserted. I searched the streets, the houses, the trees looking for a propitious sign or omen. There was a sacristan opening a church door as though for me. I gave way to an ancient impulse, got out of the car and went in. I wanted to make up a kind of prayer, an invocation making me worthy of help—one never knows. Strangely, given the early morning hour, the church was all illuminated and in the middle was a tomb and hundreds of flaming candles. A bald man kneeling near the coffin was crying, his face covered by his handkerchief. I ran back out to the car making hand signs to ward off evil, from my feet to a meter above my head.

I wanted to ask you before, and the episode you just told me offers an opportunity: where are you in relation to religion?

I would like to answer you concisely without shifting into the usual tales which depict me as a child seized by fear and terror in the icy corridors of the Salesians, in immense rooms with a hundred cots lit only by a tiny red lamp above a dark opening like the door of hell, beyond which an immense staircase led down into other corridors and salons filled only with enormous portraits of bishops; and way at the end another little door opened directly into the church where once a week before dawn we children would come to kneel in almost total darkness, and each in a high voice had to shout out his sins. If I begin to talk about that I won't finish, because I very much enjoy at least the memory of that menacing, fearsome, at times truly terrifying atmosphere. Catholicism is a good religion, considering it with detachment: it instills in you the fear of something always lying in ambush, watching you, spying on you. If it is true that religion in part liberates man from fear, in another part it powerfully generates fear. The myths of each civilization tell us of fear of the gods. Therefore God must be someone terrifying who imposes fear, being hidden and unknown. It makes sense that anything unknown grips you with fear.

I believe I am naturally religious, since to me the world and life seem wrapped in mystery. And even if I hadn't been fascinated as a child with that mystic feeling that penetrates existence and makes everything unknowable, I think the profession I practise would have led me naturally to religious sentiment. I create a dream, or rather with open eyes I abandon myself to imagining something. Then I sign a contract, and with some pieces of

87

wood, two beautiful girls, and a pair of reflectors
I make that fantasy come to life. Then everyone
can see it as I saw it while sleeping or when my
mind was blank. Who guides us through the
creative adventure? How could it happen? Only
faith in something, or someone, hidden within us,
can inspire the mysterious work of creation—
someone little known, a wise and subtle part of us,
working within us. We help that unknown part by
trusting in it, by accepting it, by letting it work for
us. That feeling of trust, I think, can be defined
as religious feeling.

On the other hand the arrogance of erudition,
of egoism, and the obsession to know more is a
false belief that often blocks out faith, stifles it,
dissolves it, almost always with less satisfying
results.

How do those ideas fit in with the Catholic Church?
That is a question to refer to Mohammed, to
Luther, or the head of some other church.

What can I answer? I have already told you that
I like it, and being born in Italy how could I have
chosen any other religion? I love its choreography,
its changeless hypnotic scenes, its precious settings,
its gloomy songs, the catechism, the election of a
new pope, the sumptuous machinery of death. I
have a feeling of gratitude for all the distortions,

the obscurities, the taboos which have created an immense body of dialectic as a basis for life-giving rebellions. And an effort to free one's self from all of those things can also give meaning to life.

But apart from those personal evaluations, the Church offers a pattern of thought which protects us from the devouring whirlpool of the unconscious. Catholic thought, like that of Islam or Hindu, is an intellectual edifice which, by establishing a code of conduct, tries to give us a compass, an orientation to guide us through the mystery of existence: a blueprint for the mind which can save us from the existential horror of loss of meaning.

I should also add that, perhaps because of atavistic memories, the Catholic Church has a dazzling attraction for me because it has been the greatest stimulator of artists—a stern mother and a watchful, generous wholesaler of exclusive masterpieces. I know it's a bit ridiculous to imagine De Laurentiis in a cardinal's vestments, but I like to think that film producers, like editors, have inherited without deserving it a kind of investiture, since the fate of the artist is to live off the bread of the grand duke, the prince, and the pope. There is a kind of artist willing to settle for freedom within the limits established by those in charge. In that way he can even feel relieved of all sense of guilt while painting, for example, a crucifix. The contract

89

that I sign with a producer is for me a substitute for the white vestments of the pope.

How do you pray?

I see that the questions are becoming bit by bit more solemn and slightly inquisitorial. Has my trial begun? However, I'll try to answer you. I think it happens to all of us, even several times a day, to murmur with stiffened lips, instead of swearing, that what is worrying us may turn out well. But perhaps that isn't praying. A similar approach, my way of praying, is to recognize particularly complicated situations from which I can't escape: suddenly I stop racking my brains, give it up, and wash my hands of it pretending the issue now concerns somebody else. "Clear out," I say, "let someone else think about it. I don't know how to settle it." And usually the issue takes care of itself.

I Vitelloni. *What comes into your mind? What links you to that film? What image connects you to it?*

I Vitelloni from hindsight: that embarcadero jutting out into the sea, a grey winter sea and a low dense cloudy sky; my brother, his hand on his hat to keep the wind from carrying it away; Leopoldo Trieste's little scarf which blew into Moraldo's face; the noise of the surf, the cries of the sea gulls. At the end even I remained hung up on that setting which became a kind of symbolic image, a poster. Then the giant face of Majeroni—Achille Majeroni who played the part of the crazy old homosexual actor who lusts after Leopoldo, the intellectual Vitellone.

Majeroni, Febo Mari, Gustavo Giorgi, Moissi: those were the signatures written in ornate calligraphy on the large photographs of the cast characters, their expressions serious, their hair long and flowing, at times reaching almost to their shoulders just like Achille Majeroni's in the play *Specters*. These regal romantic faces suddenly appeared one winter morning, just before carnival as usual, on the facades of houses, in the windows of the Commerce Cafe, at the Piazza, at the railroad station. And from there they stared at us unseeing, like unreachable divinities, promising with only the ghost of a smile that should we come to see them they would come to life. A gift of the gods to our poor sleepy forgotten village.

I really thought of them as supernatural beings, another race. And the Golden Lion Hotel which housed them for several nights took on the mythical dimensions of Mount Olympus. Everybody envied the concierge who could see them close up, could speak to them, could hand them their keys. I still couldn't imagine what the life of an actor behind the scenes or behind the blank movie screen might

91

be. I had the good luck to see Majeroni standing at the counter of a pastry shop, wearing a large white silk scarf, a pearl grey hat on his head, extremely pale, eyes almost shut, still wearing a trace of makeup, sipping through a straw something smoking in a little glass with a silver handle. Mandarin punch, the waiter told us later.

I thus got some idea from Majeroni of what his life behind the scenes might be, but the others, all the others, where did they go when the great red curtain blotted out the wonders and the lights went on in the theater callously exposing our ordinary faces? That vague impression of their unreal lives still sticks with me today in my dealings with actors. And I don't mind it. It seems better suited to my work, seems to help me understand them better, on a more secret level. I have never had problems with actors. I like their faults, their vanity, their neurotic traits, their sometimes childish, sometimes schizoid psychology. I am very grateful for what they have done for me and am always a little astonished that the airy fantasies which I have imagined for months now come alive, are flesh and blood, speaking, moving, smoking, doing what I tell them, saying their lines just as I had imagined when little by little I gave them birth.

I consider comic actors the benefactors of humankind. To give amusement, lightness, good humor, laughter—what a marvelous job. I would have liked to have been born with so happy a fate. Stan Laurel, Keaton, Oliver Hardy, Chaplin were my idols. I don't agree at all with attempts to compare Greta Garbo, Gary Cooper, Clark Gable with the flair and the talent of my marvelous clowns. A meeting with the Marx brothers left me as if struck by lightning. In a classroom theme once, while discussing the Proci who usurped Ulysses' throne while he was wandering the seas, I managed, I don't quite know how, to insert the Marx brothers. And I stoically endured the puzzled glance, a mixture of anger and disgust, that the Italian professor gave me, pushing his glasses up on his forehead. I even like the lesser comedians: the Ritz brothers, Abbott and Costello, Ben Turpin. The simple fact that they were comics gives them high marks so far as I am concerned. As a child I thought I looked a little bit like Harold Lloyd, and I would put on my father's eyeglasses, removing the lenses, in order to resemble him even more.

Actors you would have liked to work with? Is there anyone you wanted on your set who for some reason you couldn't get?

I always select an actor to match up with the character portrayed, and if I don't find one I prefer to take a person who has the right face for that character, that type, even if I have to work hard to make him become that character naturally. I have always worked with actors whom I wanted. But taking your question as an invitation to fantasize, I'll tell you the first ones who come into my mind: Mae West, with that haughty walk, that round, gluttonous baby face made satisfied, then once again gluttonous; Groucho Marx and Harpo. Our own Benigni is an exciting character, a Tuscan urchin, malicious and disrespectful, a cool little clown, moonstruck and earthy, who can take on any dimension and make it believable, from Plautus to the fairy tales of Hans Christian Andersen. Of all the comic actors of the new generation he seems to me the most original and gifted, the closest to becoming a truly stylized, indelible character.

De Sica. Vittorio De Sica, there: he comes to mind now with regard to *I Vitelloni*. I thought of him at first for the part my Majeroni later played. To tell the truth it wasn't my idea but my producer's, Pegoraro, who looked at me with pleading eyes: "There's not one big name in this film! Fellini, you're heading for a commercial disaster like *The White Sheik*. Sordi makes the public run away. Leopoldo Trieste who you're stubbornly bringing back once again is a nothing! At least agree with me in this: take De Sica for that part! Convince him, go talk to him, don't ruin me!" He covered his face with his hands and bent over on the table, sobbing.

So one winter night I went to find De Sica, who was shooting *Railroad Station*. My appointment was for after midnight in a first class train located on an unused track far away from the walkways. I had to walk laboriously across wet stones, the tracks damp with fog, fearful that every light in the darkness could be that of an arriving train. The little man who guided me talked without stopping in the tones of someone conducting me to the Pope. He would have gone up to the coach first to see if perhaps the "Commander" might be sleeping, in which case I would have to wait until he awoke. "If I have to, I'll throw a stone at the window." But I didn't have to. De Sica was awake there in the dark shadows of his first class compartment, and he benevolently motioned me to enter.

I had never seen him close up before. He held the velvet-silver charm of his character under full control. Even his voice, flute-like and slightly throaty, was as always. De Sica, like Toto the clown, managed to maintain even in real life that airy unreachable quality which makes certain people seem to be seen as if through the magic depths of a mirror, enchanting, unattainable. He was most likeable, using charm like a profession, like a philosophy that says: be likeable and you shall be forgiven much. De Sica was likeable even when he was proclaimed the Italian poet of war, of ruin and misery, at which time he took on a thoughtful immobility and a tone of voice thick with bitter knowledge.

Seated in front of him in the darkness of the compartment, in a padded unreal atmosphere, I described with some emotion the character I wanted him to play. A great dramatic actor, I explained, a great actor who has been famous but who life has now forced to make painful compromises, playing in a small company with second billing. "One night this little company arrives at an obscure town in the provinces, where a young man full of dreams and literary ambitions asks the once famous actor to listen to the reading of a play of his, and the actor consents." De Sica smiled sympathetically, approvingly, and murmured something about youth. Encouraged I went on with the story up to the scene where the lecherous old man reveals his intentions to the naive playwright-Vitellone. De Sica, who perhaps was dozing off for a fraction of a second, continued to smile benevolently. Suddenly he seemed to understand, stared at me surprised, perplexed. "You mean that he has other aspects, another purpose?" Then, after a slight hesitation, in a low voice: "Gay?" I nodded yes, a little embarrassed. There was a rather long silence. De Sica looked out the window. Silence. "But—he finally said looking bravely at me—human?" "Most human," I hastened to declare. De Sica nodded rapidly, agreeing with his thoughts, biting his inner lip. Then again with his beautiful musical voice he affirmed: "Because gays can have great humanity, more than we might suspect." "Certainly." I said, "No doubt about it!"

Someone from the production crew entered obsequiously to notify us that the lighting was set and the actors in place. De Sica got up, adjusted the scarf around his neck, extended to me a beautiful soft warm large hand: "Bravo, a superb character. I like him. Make an appointment with my lawyer. We'll talk about it. But remember, human!"

For reasons that I don't remember it wasn't possible to sign De Sica, and perhaps it was better that way. The character created by De Sica would have been too sympathetic, too interesting, too entertaining. And perhaps the public would have misunderstood and perhaps disapproved of Leopoldo's bewilderment and flight into the darkness of the quay, when with a sweet and inviting voice the old actor tries to coax him to follow him to a more solitary and out of the way place.

What advice would you give a young man who wants to be an actor?

I really wouldn't know what to tell him. Usually I just look him in the eye silently, much more embarrassed than he is. It seems to me I am the person least suited to give advice or directions, to suggest techniques, behavior, discipline. In general I do not follow a system in my own work, which is all the more reason why I can't provide one for others. Also my choice of actors is somewhat unique in the sense that despite all the esteem, sympathy, involvement that I always feel toward actors, when I get ready to choose one to be a character in one of my films I am not attracted by his talent in the normal sense of the term: that is, professional competence. Similarly, in selecting a non-actor I am not bothered by his lack of experience. For me the character and the actor must coincide. I go in search of faces that say everything about themselves upon their first appearance on the screen. I tend to underscore character, to reveal it with makeup, with costume, the way a mask makes all things crystal clear— conduct, psychology, destiny. The choice of the actor for the character I have in mind depends on the face I see before me, what it communicates to me and also what it permits me to intuit, to recognize, to sense underneath. I don't require the interpreter to doll up like somebody else. I want him to express what best suits him. That way the result is always positive. Everyone has a face that can only be his, with no other one possible. And the faces are always just right. Life does not make mistakes.

Besides actors faces, how do you deal with the materials you use? I would like you to tell me about the artistic part of your work, about your method of translating fantasy into pictures, about "Making a Film," to quote the title of one of your books.

You're asking me to reveal shop secrets which I don't have, or don't think I have in as programmed a form, in as pharmaceutical doses, as your question implies. Not everything can be gathered up into alchemical formulas, into mathematical combinations of ingredients which insure the right prescription, the efficient dosage. It isn't that I want to cloak the key to expression in mystery, as some do. It's just impossible to explain, at least for me, in a full and responsible way. Would it make sense for me to enumerate with absolute precision, like in a ledger, how many meters of silk, how many of cloth, how many nails, decorations, costumes, how many made-up faces are needed to translate into a film scene the vague, fluctuating, fascinating image—made so by its being indeterminate—that

I used as source material? And all the other thousands of happenings that made this scene possible: the movements, dimensions, perspectives, the tones of voice in certain dialects, the rhythms, musical themes, focus, shadows, opposing light, chiaroscuro, and who knows how many other elements and tensions, stimulating doubts, terrors, enthusiasms? I would have to try to write a dissertation, to examine myself from top to bottom, to look inside myself with ridiculous pettiness—and then? I'm sure I still wouldn't manage to isolate everything that went into composing that single unique frame, still wouldn't succeed in pulling out, in reconstructing that unreachable indescribable mysterious component which brings everything together at the end apart from my logic, my premises, good will, talent, artistic sense. I could never succeed in dissecting that moment of magnetic fusion which gives unity and credibility to the whole kaboodle while still retaining the illusion, the seductiveness, the symbolism, of the fantasized image.

What attention have you paid in your films to scenic values over the course of the years? And to sound?
At the beginning I probably suppressed the narrative aspect of dialogue and made films more along literary lines and less supple and malleable.

As I progressed I acquired more faith in images and increasingly tried to do less with words while filming. During the dubbing I return to giving considerable importance to dialogue. In this I am different from Antonioni who sometimes, in order to express everything via image, concentrates obsessively, monotonously on objects. I feel a need to give sound the same expressive quality as image, to create a kind of sight and sound polyphony. And since they are opposites, I oppose using the face and voice of the same actor. The important thing is that the character have a voice that makes him even more expressive. For me dubbing is indispensable, a kind of musical activity which reinforces what the characters mean. Direct takes don't work for me. The multiple sounds in direct takes are useless. In my films, for example, footsteps are almost never heard. Those are sounds the spectator adds with his mind's eye and need no underscoring. If the spectator really heard them they would bother him. That is why the sound track is a job to do separately, after all the rest, along with the music.

The play of invention, the magic of creation... In your sensual search for the absolute there is a good deal of mysticism.

Film is a divine way of telling about life, of paralleling God the Father! No other profession lets you create a world which comes so close to the one we know, as well as to unknown, parallel, concentric ones.

For me the ideal place—I have said this many times—is Theater 5 in Cinecittà when it's empty. Total emotion, trembling, ecstasy is what I feel there in that empty studio—a space to fill up, a world to create.

The extremes of squalor and nakedness are the breath of life to me. I have the absolute conviction of being a demiurge. I would even be happy filming passport photographs, portraits of the gentry, anything. I am not bound to any style. I like them all. I have a great love for my work and it seems to me that everything else—relationships with other people, transitory feelings, periodic alliances—all come together in this alembic. I feel it as the most authentic thing in my life, without question or denial. I obey its call. The highest peak of love or the most excruciating tension are one and the same: a mysterious moment, a perpetual illusion, the hope that at one time or another the promise of a supreme revelation will be kept and a message will appear in letters of fire. In myth, the magician and the virgin actually come together. The magician needs this feminine figure intact in order to master knowledge. And the same thing happens to the artist who, in a much more modest way, at the moment his creation comes to life, embraces its expression.

Between I Vitelloni *and* La Strada *there is* Matrimonial Agency, *one of the episodes of* Love in the City. *Have you ever seen it again?*

I saw a little of it one evening in a bar I went into to make a phone call. In a little back room lighted only by a TV set there was someone watching. I didn't hear the sound, I only saw Cifariello, one of the actors in the piece, seated on a grassy bank talking to the comic pathetic young girl ready to marry the wolf man. I was tempted to edge my way into the little room and stand there watching some sequences of that film which I really remember nothing about. But then one of the scruffy spectators with the remote control switch in his hand suddenly changed the station.

It was Cesare Zavattini who made me the offer to contribute an episode to this film which was to be like straight reporting, in the style of American films. Marco Ferreri was production director, and at that time he was trying to lose weight, claiming he didn't want any snacks. But then during breaks he went from one to the other of us looking like a starving bum. We all gave him something, so he ended up eating ten snacks.

I agreed to participate in that collective film with all the competitive spirit of a young student grumpily accepting his professor's jokes. *I Vitelloni* had had a great success but left the left wing critics cold and distant. Though the consensus was positive, they were critical about my locating the film in a nameless province and accused me of overemphasizing poetic memory and not knowing how to give a film a clear political meaning. I thought I'd take a little revenge on those who made knee jerk statements in favor of neorealism during those years, thus creating the abominable consequences which still persist.

What would be the abominable consequences of Rossellini's neorealistic teachings?

That was hardly the intention of Rossellini's neorealism, which avoids at its peril the sloppy and the casual. The primary requisite for making a neorealistic film is respect for realism at all costs as an existential, unalterable, untouchable sacred happening. Personal feeling, subjective thrusts, the need to select, to express the artistic sense, are subject here to politics: down with memory, interpretation, points of view stimulated by feeling; down with fantasy; punish the author! Idleness, ignorance and laziness have made the new aesthetic accepted enthusiastically. Anyone can make films; everyone should make them—a non-aesthetic aesthetic which I think has contributed in large part to the present crisis of our cinema.

I invented a matrimonial agency nestled in the attic of an enormous tumble-down palace and the story of a young girl who, in order to marry, had to accept matrimony with a wolf man. I swore that it was all real, and when I showed the first montage of my episode the left wing film critics came to me fully satisfied: "Have you observed, dear Fellini, how reality is always more fantastic than the most unbridled fantasy?"

After that joke La Strada *finally arrived. Thinking about it today, what does that film represent for you?*
A phrase by critic Pietrino Bianchi comes to mind. I don't remember if he wrote it in a newspaper or in a book of his collected reviews or whether he told it to me directly. The film was shown at the Venice Festival to a positive, even enthusiastic consensus (the French critics were particularly favorable: kisses, handshakes, "Your film is already a classic," said Cayatte, and little André Bazin, as thin as St. Francis, agreed, eyeing me like a benediction)—on the other side was total opposition by most of the left wing journalists. In the midst of that exciting, tumultuous, contrasting reception it seemed to me that Pietrino Bianchi's comment differed from all the others: "What a courageous film!" he said. And thinking it over today it seems to me that at that moment, at least, his judgment was the fairest.

La Strada: Anthony Quinn and Giulietta Masina

La Strada: Giulietta Masina

La Strada was a film that presented the most profound contrasts: unhappiness and nostalgia, plus a feeling of time running out, which therefore couldn't relate to social and political problems. In neorealistic terms, *La Strada* was a film of rejection, decadent and reactionary. It seems to me that Bianchi made clear my courage in going against the current in that film.

But my memories of *La Strada* are too full, and I want to get rid of them. To evoke them would soon put me in the embarrassing situation of recreating *Lives of the Saints*, given the unique destiny of that film which traveled all around the world trailing a kind of ecumenical charisma.

Wouldn't you want to at least tell me how the idea of La Strada *was born?*

How can you really put your fingers on the moment of first contact with the feeling, or better yet the presentiment, the anticipation of what will then become your film? The roots from which Gelsomina and Zampano were born and their story reach deep into a profound and dark place populated by a sense of guilt, by fear, by melting nostalgia for a higher morality, by regret for innocence betrayed. I don't feel like talking about it. Everything I say would seem out of proportion and useless.

I seem to remember hazily that I was driving my car past the fields around Rome in that lazy relaxed way I have of wandering, which perhaps made me catch a glimpse of the characters, the feeling, the atmosphere of that film for the first time.

Speaking of cars, it seems to me that now you don't use them any more, but before your passion for custom made cars was famous.

I haven't had a car for some ten years now. One day I suddenly decided to get rid of them. There was a beautiful Mercedes, metallic green with glints of gold, two-door, automatic transmission with three forward speeds, convertible: better yet, by pushing a button a flap on the roof opened up and if I wanted I could drive standing up, making benedictions in full view. But one day at Riccione a kid eight or nine years old in a little Fiat was coming out of a one-way street against a red light, and he ran into me at a crossroads. Everybody sitting at the outdoor cafe—it was summer time— irrationally and against all evidence said the kid was right, even the policeman. I decided then and there to get rid of the car. There was a German among the bystanders who, when he heard the policeman say my name, told me he wanted to give his wife, in Hamburg, an anniversary gift two months from now. He thought that giving her the car of the director of *La Dolce Vita* would represent the height of love and devotion. I liked the idea of selling a Mercedes to a German, and we concluded the deal with a handshake at that crossroads, under a traffic light, in front of the juvenile delinquent and the crowd, which then applauded.

Perhaps the time had come. I was fed up with cars: too many problems, too many fines, too many no parking signs, too many taxes, the garage too far away, and above all too many killing stares from assassins and from loonies in other cars who sometimes would catch up to me and ride alongside me in town. I don't regret the lack of a car at all. There are taxis (I like to sit in the front and chat with the drivers), automobiles used for productions of my films, and all my friends have cars—there's always someone willing to take me.

And when I don't find anyone and it begins to rain I stand in the middle of the street peering into the cars coming towards me. And I shamelessly pretend to make a mistake and greet someone as if it's someone I know. A car always stops and the driver, male or female, graciously offers me a ride.

I have had the most beautiful expensive extravagant cars. I remember a sky blue Studebaker which seemed like a tri-motor airplane, a spaceship. When I drove slowly through the countryside around Rome with that car the locals would tip their

hats and many of them bowed. We made a contest,
Marcello Mastroianni and I, out of buying new cars.
He bought a Jaguar? I a Triumph! He a Triumph?
I a Porsche. Marcello a Porsche too? I a BMW.
Our tiresome underhanded game made Bornigia,
the old car dealer, rich. He changed suits every day,
each one more elegant, always more expensive, and
was able to do so with all the money that old
"Snaporaz" and I gave him.

I couldn't begin to tell you of the feelings and
fantasies connected with that first little Fiat
Rossellini gave me as compensation for a script he
never paid me for. I couldn't begin to tell you all
the cars I've had. I only remember those that I liked
the most: the Alfa Romeo 1910 seemed to me the
most elegant and the best designed, and I don't
understand why they discontinued production on
that popular model. I also very much liked the
Mercedes Pagodina and the Lancia Flaminia, even
if when driving it I felt like the chauffeur of a
minister of state.

By car I discovered fabulous Latium, the villages
perched on top of hills, the countryside, the
threshing floors in full sunlight, the fabulous
Maccarese region that seemed like the Medieval
Japan in films of Kurosawa, and many other things
as well. To my wanderings by car through town
and country and along the sea I especially owe the

first glimmerings of my films, ideas, characters, even dialogues. I would often stop wherever I was and take notes. That floating wandering without a goal past things, colors, trees, sky, and the faces that silently filed by the windows of the car have always had the power to gather me up into an indefinable still point, where images, feelings, and intuitions are spontaneously born.

To get back to your films: in 1953 you made La Strada, *the next year* Il Bidone *[The Swindle]. Am I mistaken, or did your early films follow one another more rapidly. In other words it seems to me you were more productive then, making a film a year.*

My great regret is not being able to work all the time, with the continuity, the joyous energetic speed, the fast lane through which I moved in the 1950's. The financial structure of my films has grown heavier and heavier and created gigantic appetites, a kind of hypertrophy certainly not caused by me, but which has made the whole process more complicated and troublesome.

If on the one hand I have been lucky because I've always managed to make the films I wanted, the way I wanted, and with the least frictions and compromises, on the other hand I regret not having met in all these years a traveling companion, a great impresario willing to program my work and to

protect me from all the going astray into which
vanity or curiosity or impatience has led me at times
for good or evil. I have not had the good fortune
of a fateful meeting with someone who could make
suggestions and with whom I can even argue, like
that indispensable rapport between painter and
pope, between court poet and grand duke.

When an American producer lets me know that
he wants to meet with me at the Grand Hotel or
at the Excelsior to discuss a film, a project to be
carried out in the United States, I always arrive
punctually at the meeting even though I know I
will never go to America. I don't like to delude him,
but I am curious to hear what he has to say, and
that way I get involved. I lose months not doing
what I should do: standing in the studio and saying,
"Camera!"

*Fellini in America: will you end up one time or
another going there to shoot a film?"*

I could have made several films in America had
I wanted, but in truth I don't know if I can. De
Laurentiis, who has been there for many years, calls
me twice a month at three or four in the morning
pretending not to know the existence of time zones.
He has offered to let me direct practically all the
films he's made there, from *King Kong* to *Flash
Gordon*, but I have always shilly-shallied and at the

end said no. Even though to tell the truth I am convinced I would have enjoyed making a fine psychoanalytic story like *King Kong*. Because on a Pacific island or in a California studio the temptation to give into American realism would not arise. I told Dino after that film came out that I would gladly have made it. I barely had time to finish the sentence when with a shout of joy he said, "Bravo Fefe! God has lighted your way! Let's make *The Daughter of King Kong* immediately!" And fool that I am, that time I said no...

I doubt that I will ever manage to make a film in America. They invite me to go there, to be there twelve or fifteen weeks and as a result of that experience develop ideas. Kind and gracious American friends want to host me, to put at my disposal their houses, their time, their scenic spectacles, their writers, trips from coast to coast! They tell me I can visit their great cities and regions and ask to see anything I want, that I'll be totally taken care of. I will even meet with artists, learned men, anyone I'd enjoy meeting, from Norman Mailer to Woody Allen to Truman Capote to that fascinating gentle specter, Andy Warhol. They would definitely show me the things, places, people they judge most "Fellini-like," which would totally embarrass me. The result of all that could only be to give it up, to withdraw, and in an uneasy attempt to justify myself explain to them that I am not capable, that I don't know how to make a film in America. Because even though their country fascinates me, seduces me and seems like an immense set congenial to my vision of things, I wouldn't know how to tell it in a film. New York! It is stupendous, an immense spaceship liberated in the cosmos. It has no roots or depth, but suspended on an infinite crystal dish it is Ninevah, Venice, Damascus, Benares, all the cities of the world merged together in a dazzling futuristic decadent stage set. New York is sweet, violent, beautiful, terrific: but how can I narrate it? Only here in my own country could I attempt such a titanic undertaking, at Cinecittà, in the hovel of Theater 5. Whatever risk I take there I am always protected from falling off the cliff by the capacious net consisting of my roots, my memories, my habits, my home: in sum, by my laboratory. Besides, it is one thing to live in, to be moved by, to have sensations and feel things about a new reality. All of us can certainly do that, can see it, exalt it, marvel at it. We all feel an impact, a stimulus, a rapport with things we do not know. But to tell about them, to express them, to restate them believably and vividly without mistakes or misunderstandings can only be done by expressing them in our own language. That is the only means we have at our disposal to communicate with ourselves before doing so with others. The misunderstanding comes from the fact that people think of cinema as a camera loaded with film and a reality out there all ready to be photographed. Instead, one inserts himself between the object and the camera. Otherwise a film can only offer vaguely contradictory information. In America ideas come to me across a language that is not my own, across a reality whose allusions I do not know and which escape from me into their own stratified levels and into the components of their own roots. My filmmaking is work that requires a total mastery of language to produce a vision of the world, its myths, its collective imagination. I surely don't pretend to know everything about Italy, but at least here I invoke *my* ignorance, *my* emotions. Here I am the master even of the things I don't know. I can say that someone is from Bergamo by looking at his necktie. Well, maybe that's a little exaggerated. But as regards Italian reality I have the illusion of understanding the relationships among the different systems of representation, among newspapers, television, publicity, winks of an eye, and the syntheses of images common to us all. . .

But other prestigious directors work in America without difficulty.

Yes, I know that Milos Forman, Roman Polanski and many others have succeeded in participating fully in American culture and in expressing it. But they come from a different world; they are Jews, middle Europeans. They come from a psychological and cultural dimension which has habituated them to become everywhere more native than the natives. They have always had a special talent that allows them to absorb like vampires the history, culture, memories of others. They have truly become more American than the Americans.

Twenty-five years ago I signed up for a project with three enthusiastic American producers who decided to get away from the major companies and their politics and to make Italian type films. Neorealism had caught them up, excited them, and they even wanted to get out of the studios and tell real stories with real people "off the street," as the saying went at that time. I was in Los Angeles for the Oscars, and the three producers eyed me approvingly. They liked everything about me, not only *I Vitelloni* and *La Strada* but also my neckties, my hair style, the way I spoke English. One time I banged my knee against the corner of a piece of furniture—no big deal, only a little pain. Well, I had to start screaming to prevent them from taking me to the hospital and, who knows, being operated on immediately.

With great reluctance I agreed to sign a contract which projected a stay of twelve weeks in America, after which I was to be ready to shoot a film or else go home. They were quite certain that this second possibility would never happen.

Thus I began my wanderings around the United States. They put at my disposal secretaries, interpreters, friends, journalists, and a most likeable picturesque mafioso named Serenella. He must have been seventy years old, but powerful and vigorous with the dark features of an ancient gladiator and heavily pockmarked cheeks. His white hair, instead of giving him an air of nobility made him look even more shifty. He was terribly sentimental. Just looking at me moved him. A tough but sweet grandfather who removed his gloves when he stroked my head. He had tremendous influence which sometimes frightened me a little. Everything I asked him for was immediately taken care of; there were no limits. I would want to see this, I would want to visit that, can I take a walk with Mae West? Joan Blondell? Jane Russell?—even impossible things that I asked him just to provoke him. He was a big time boss with two hotels in Las Vegas, admired and feared, and when he hummed Gelsomina's theme he would blow his nose and point to his fierce bloodshot eyes now veiled with tears. . . But after a month I ached with homesickness. I passed whole afternoons locked in the hotel telephoning all my friends in Rome, even mere acquaintances and even people I'd broken with years ago. I was homesick for little things—it was torture—like going out to buy the newspapers at night on Cola di Rienzo Avenue or going into the shadowy, churchlike Plaza Hotel just to make a phone call, or loafing idly around bookstores.

I liked America a great deal. It seduced me, fascinated me. It seemed to me that everything there was ready-made, like a huge prefabricated set with perfect scenery, its lighting and layout tailor-made. A lot of ideas came to me, and when I told them to my producers they were enthusiastic. "That's it!" they would say, "Terrific!" But I felt it was not possible to experience something and narrate it, to live it and express it, immediately. I don't have the talent or vocation of a journalist. My chances of communicating through verisimilitude are almost nonexistent. Besides I believe I can be a good reporter only if I invent things. Therefore, acting like a fragile neurotic young girl, I said that I wanted to go home after only four weeks, that I didn't remember how to be a director any more, that I didn't know how to make films any more. Serenella with his black floppy hat, his flowing white silk scarf, and his coat with the velvet

collar in pure George Raft style, accompanied me
to the airport. He said nothing; no comment. He
accepted my decision and respected it, convinced
that if I had decided that way, it meant there was
something more interesting for me, more advan-
tageous, "more money" if I went somewhere else.
At the last moment before leaving he gave me the
address of a friend of his who had been deported
from the United States as an "undesirable" and who
was now in Italy. (No, I don't want to give you his
name, and besides he's not there any more.) "He's
a saint!" Serenella told me, "He has done good for
everybody, but they didn't understand him. My
dear boy, if you need him, go to him and kiss him
for me." I didn't go to him, didn't bring him kisses
from Serenella in spite of a great curiosity to know
this saintly man. A couple of times, in the face of
great difficulty getting a film started, I found myself
looking at the note that the worthy, sinister old man
gave me. But then the next day perhaps when, who
knows . . . like, in comes my friend Peppino Amato
saying in his blustering way: "I'll make it, *La Dolce
Vita*! It'll be a super success! Sign here! After it's
done you'll go back with me to America and, you'll
see, when the Americans see us they will all
salaam!"

Are you more at home in Eastern Europe?

To me Eastern Europe seems like Gambettola, the countryside near Rimini where my grandmother lived. The Russian way of kissing and holding you by the hands before greeting you has always seemed to me a sign of that rural religious feeling I breathed in my grandmother's house during holy week, along with the scent of certain sweets. When I've been in Russia I have been especially aware of this deja vu, this sense of Christian existence which echoes Tolstoy more than Mayakovsky. It brings back memories of a life framed between earth and sky, marked by long intertwining seasons and sweetened by scents and flavors of earlier times; memories from when I was little and my senses delighted in all the things around me, people, plants, trees, the smell of houses. . . That dimension which at daybreak links man to the earth, to changes in the atmosphere, to the clouds, to a sense of brotherhood, to small rituals, to recurrences, to holidays, to gratitude toward the someone who has gifted you with all that. Naturally a good part of those thoughts also stem from literature, but then you realize, like everyone, that in a sense those things are exactly what you perceive them to be.

Evtushenko, whom I first met during the premiere of *8½* at the Moscow festival, instantly

121

seemed like a friend from school. They introduced us and everyone surrounded us, journalists, photographers, everybody waiting for the important things we would say. The interpreters hung on our every word, but we didn't know the correct things to say of historic or decisive importance. We just simply liked one another. When, years later, he came to look me up at Fregene we talked together like old friends. He had learned Italian in three days. On the beach one night he told me that in Greenland one winter evening—one of those evenings that lasts six months—an Eskimo with a movie projector on a boat in the middle of the ice showed *Nights of Cabiria*. Everybody enjoyed and was moved by it, even the polar bears. Then he said something beautiful which always comes to mind when I think of Evtushenko: he said that seals have a moist tender glance like that of his wife. Now I don't know if it pleases a woman to hear that she has eyes like a seal. But from that time on I've looked at seals differently. And it's true: they do have very beautiful eyes with a tormenting sweetness that makes you feel guilty.

Walking along the bank we outdistanced our friends whose voices we heard behind us in the dark. Summer had not yet begun. It was a most beautiful night, a bit cool, and Sergei suddenly stripped to his shorts while reciting poetry and jumped into the water. I lost sight of him, and when the others caught up they reproached me and told me I shouldn't have allowed him to do that. They all called out: "Evtushenko!" but up ahead there was only total darkness, a few far off gleams and an immense stretch of water mingling with the starlight...What should we do? Phone the port officials? The Russian ambassador? Khrushchev? Someone was already weeping and saying, "He was a great poet!" To tell the truth we were all thinking the worst, because an hour had already passed since his disappearance. We had decided to organize rescue squads when lo and behold, out he came from the darkness along the bank. He had had a great swim and after two kilometers was coming back by land. Now he wanted to know if I thought Tasso or Ariosto was the greater poet. What a glorious *Vitellone*! A real childhood companion!

But why all this to describe whether I feel more at home in Eastern Europe? As accustomed as we are in Italy to giving away our freedom, which at times we've actually been convinced is too much for us, I don't think we will have the energy or patience to support the degrading dullness, the censorous zeal of a communist regime.

When *Amarcord* was to be shown in Russia I was invited to the Russian Embassy in Rome for a talk. There was caviar, vodka and a gracious and

123

impenetrable minister who wanted me to agree to
cuts in the film. I didn't understand why, or what
cuts had to be made, and naturally I opposed them.
"The minister asks—translated the interpreter—
why you want to deprive the Russian people of your
film." "Indeed I don't want to. I am even happy
that my film is coming out in the Soviet Union."
The interpreter transmitted the message, listened,
and then turned back to me: "Then you must cut
out the scene in the tobacco shop." "Is the minister
himself disturbed by the saleswoman's tits?" I
asked. The interpreter, a little flustered, translated
and then hastened to reassure me: "No, not at all!"
The minister too shook his head reassuringly, his
expression solemn. "Then may I know—I
insisted—why the Russian audience should be
considered different from the minister? If it's all
right for one, it should be all right for the others!"
The discussion continued that way for a while, with
the interpreter more and more embarrassed at
having to translate my arguments and the minister
insisting that I shouldn't want to deprive the Soviet
people of the joy of seeing my film. At the end I
left with my presents of vodka and caviar, the
smiles of everyone, and the greatest assurances of
esteem and admiration. But *Amarcord* shown in
Russia came out with the tobacconist scene
mutilated and also the scene in which the boys

masturbated in an old automobile. The Russian people were not deprived of my film, only of some of its value. That censorous restrictive authoritarian side—more so than the confessional and more obscurantist than the Church—makes togetherness out of the question.

Have you ever had trouble with Italian censorship? As I remember, Nights of Cabiria *provoked many protests in Catholic circles.*

The censor forbade its showing and I didn't want them to burn the negatives. Therefore following the advice of an intelligent, slightly less than conformist Jesuit friend, Father Arpa, I visited a famous cardinal in Genoa, considered one of the leading church authorities and rather powerful, to ask him to see the film. In a tiny projection room located behind the harbor I centered an armchair bought the day before from an antique dealer, a sort of throne with a great red cushion with gold fringes. Half an hour after midnight the cardinal arrived in his black Mercedes. I was not permitted to remain in the projection room, so I don't know whether the high churchman really saw the whole film or whether he slept; probably Father Arpa woke him up at the right moments, when there were processions or sacred images. Suffice it that he said at the end: "Poor Cabiria, we ought to do

125

Amarcord

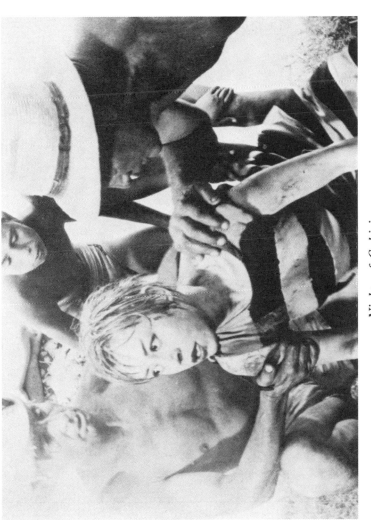

Nights of Cabiria

something for her!" I now think a simple phone call to him would have been enough.

Someone accused me publicly of being a kind of Richelieu who, instead of fighting out in the open, plotted behind the scenes. Happily in those days we had time to waste on that kind of situation. But in the end the film was saved, on one extraordinary condition, however, laid down by the cardinal: that the sequence involving the man with the sack be cut.

And what was in that sequence?

The episode was inspired by a remarkable character with whom I spent two or three nights wandering around Rome: a sort of philanthropist and somewhat of a magician who, after having had a vision dedicated himself to a peculiar mission. He gathered up the disinherited from the oddest corners of the city and gave them food and clothing, which he carried in a sack. He did this day after day.

With him I saw unlikely things. By lifting the grill of a certain sewer where there seemed to be only mud and mice, we found an old lady sleeping. In the corridors of a sumptuous palace on the via del Corso, where the Socialist Party now is, were bums who slept there till five in the morning, secretly let in by the night watchman. The man with the sack knew all of those places. He gave food, and even injections, in one place or another.

In the film I imagined that Cabiria met him on the Appian Way while returning home in the first light of dawn, grumbling because one lousy client hadn't paid her. She saw the man with the sack get off a petrol bike, head toward the rock quarries, stop at the edge of a sort of gulf and call a woman by name. An old whore whom Cabiria had known as the Atomic Bomb came out of that miserable ravine, reduced to leading the life of a mole. Afterward Cabiria accepted a ride home from the man with the sack and was moved by the stories he told. It was a touching sequence but I had to cut it. Apparently in certain Catholic circles it was upsetting that the film pay this kind of homage to an absolutely weird philanthropist untouched by the influence of the Church.

And isn't it ridiculous that the mayor of Rome protested when *Cabiria* came out because I had put the whores in a place—the Archaeological Promenade—which he had tried so hard to upgrade.

If the censor should abolish his codes and allow total liberty would you make a porno film?
The word implies a certain knowledge of vulgarity, and someone who is knowledgeable about

vulgarity cannot be the thing itself. I wouldn't know how to avoid that contradiction. And my customary symbolic values would transform the work in a way that probably would not please either the distributors nor that kind of public. Furthermore I have never found anyone who said, "Ah, I have seen a beautiful porno film." I have always understood that there were hideous women in them who make you feel you're in the morgue or the stockyards. You breathe the atmosphere of a whorehouse there, which means a porno film makes you feel you know less than before and are participating in a degrading collective ceremony.

You haven't spoken of Il Bidone *[The Swindle], which came before* Nights of Cabiria. *Why did you pick an American actor? Did the producer impose Broderick Crawford on you?*

I have had the pleasure and good fortune to work with producers who have never imposed anything or anyone on me. If our points of view differed we broke off the project by common consent. And even if those ruptures happened a hundred times, my relationship with all producers, the ones I made films with and those with whom I broke a contract, have remained friendly. In sum, from time immemorial we have always been on the same side about making films, and we have understood one another without illusions.

I chose Broderick Crawford after much difficulty finding the main character among many many faces. One evening in Piazza Mazzini I saw a large wall poster for a film which had been torn vertically. Half a face still showed and below it half a title and half the name of the actor: *"All the King's"* and Broderi. The little eye in that half of a fat face reminded me of the sharp, canine expression of a certain Nasi who was famous in Rimini for having sold a German a stretch of the sea in front of the Grand Hotel. At least that was the story they told about Nasi the swindler, and when anyone asked him at the Commerce Cafe to confirm whether it was true or not, Nasi would first want to be treated to a drink. After that he would utter sentences of "oriental" wisdom, such as: "We no longer know how to see the truth because we do not know how to lower ourselves to join with earth." If someone asked for an explanation of that, he first had to pay for another glass of wine. And this situation, between oracular responses and further carafes of wine, could go on the entire afternoon until the oracle, completely drunk, went off into the fog singing at the top of his lungs.

What a huge magnificent face Broderick Crawford had! Absolutely sensational testimony to the film photographer's art: he had only to raise an eyebrow and there was a story in it. Those little eyes sunk in those fat cheeks seemed to be looking at you from behind a wall, like two holes in a partition. The producer, worried about rumors circulating about Brod's love of drink, wanted a warning put in the actor's contract, plus a one page list of acceptable drinks. There still must have been some infractions on Brod's part though, because I remember one morning when we were almost at the end of the film, after about four months of his having been in Rome, his insisting more and more angrily that a production secretary go and get him Turkish cigarettes found only in one particular "tobacco shop" beyond the sixth building on Fourteenth Street.

La Dolce Vita.

I answer right away, as in word association tests: Anita Ekberg! Twenty-five years after the film, its title, its image are still inseparable from Anita.

I saw her for the first time in a full page photograph in an American magazine: a powerful panther playing the mischievous young girl, astride the banister of a stairway. "My God—I thought— don't ever let me meet her!" That sense of the marvelous, of a hypnotic stupor, of the disbelief one feels confronting exceptional creatures like the giraffe, the elephant, the baobab tree I felt again several years later when I saw her coming toward me in the garden of the Hotel de la Ville. She was preceded, followed, flanked by three or four little men, husband, agents, who disappeared like shadows around a haloed source of light—I insist that Ekberg is most of all phosphorescent. She wanted to know about the script, whether the character was good, who the other actors were, the while drinking one of those cocktails full of colors, flags and little fish from an enormous glass and speaking in a husky childlike voice that made her even more overwhelming. I seemed to be discovering the platonic reality of things, of elements, and in a total stupor I murmured to myself: "Ah, these are ear lobes, these are gums, this is human skin." That same evening, I went to see Marcello Mastroianni who listened somewhat disturbed but not wanting it to show: "Go on—he said—really? But! Oh well—he concluded in a condescending tone raising his eyebrow à la Clark Gable—let's go and see this lady!"

With her profound knowledge of men Anita, when Marcello was introduced to her, offered him her hand while absentmindedly looking elsewhere and didn't say a word to him all evening. Later Marcello, while discussing something else, mentioned that Ekberg was not so big a deal. She reminded him too much of a German soldier in the *Wehrmacht* who once during an MP round up tried

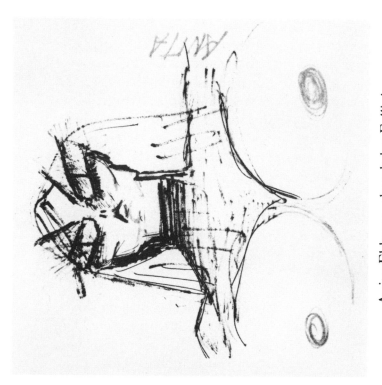

Anita Ekberg: sketch by Fellini

La Dolce Vita: Anita Ekberg

to escape in a truck. Perhaps he felt offended, disdained. Instead of making him feel exalted, that elemental glory of divinity, that healthy shark, that reflection of tropical suns had angered old "Snaporaz."

La Dolce Vita *remains a key to the vault of twentieth century culture and imagination. After more than twenty years, what do you think of it today? How much were you aware then of its sociological elements?*

Regularly deceiving friends and journalists I have always said that the Rome of *La Dolce Vita* was an internal city and that the title of the film had no moral or denigrating purpose. It simply meant to say that in spite of everything life had its profound undeniable sweetness.

I quite agree with those who maintain that the author is the last to talk knowledgeably about his work. And I don't want to appear to be someone who tends, through coquetry or exhibitionism, to demythify or diminish what he has done. But I believe I never had any specific intention to denounce, criticize, scourge, or satirize. I don't stew over protests, angers, things I can't tolerate. I'm not out to accuse anyone. Via Veneto? I never go there. I don't think I spoke even once with Flaiano about the via Veneto. The sequence with the nobles? I added that during the retakes; it was suggested by certain stories that Brunello Rondi, a frequent guest at parties and celebrations in Roman patrician houses, told me. The final orgy? Thinking Pier Paolo Pasolini was an orgy expert, I invited him to supper one night. But Pier Paolo told me right away that he was sorry but that he knew nothing about bourgeois orgies and had never participated in one. "Don't you know anyone who has?" I asked him. No, he didn't know anyone. Jacopetti? He was in Africa at that time. So I began the sequence without an idea. I relied on the actors, setting them in unconvincing attitudes of debauchery. I had a Dutch assistant, a beautiful girl, who followed me with attentive trusting eyes, excitedly waiting to see me produce who knows what outrageous turpitude. After about two hours I heard her murmur, very disillusioned: "He wants to do the dirty and he doesn't know how."

Yes, but La Dolce Vita *is also much more. It marks off a period in Italian life and has become its symbol. It has provoked discussions, debates, scandal...*

I am aware that *La Dolce Vita* constitutes a phenomenon which has gone beyond the film itself, not only beyond the view of the customs it reflects, but also because of its innovations: it was the first Italian film to last three and a half hours—even my friends wanted me to cut it. I had to defend it with everything I had. I made it the way I make all my films, in part to get rid of it, but especially because of my unshamed craving to tell stories. It seems to me that the inspiration for the film, and the formation of its images, derived from the lifestyle shown in picture magazines such as *Europeo* and *Oggi*—senseless spectacles featuring shady aristocrats, Fascism, and how those magazines photograph such spectacles and glamorize them on their pages. Those picture magazines were the troubled mirror of a society continually celebrating itself, showing itself off, praising itself: a society whose nobility is pontifical, sinister and small town, which got its start in *Caravelle* and then was photographed worldwide. It represents a reactionary seventeenth century Italy, and I enjoyed making faces at it.

But how could I explain all that to that little old lady dressed in black, with her straw hat and ribbons and lace. A couple of months after the film appeared the scandal burst. The *Osservatore Romano* wrote fiery articles against *La Dolce Vita* and its author every day and talked about withdrawing the censor's approval of the film, of burning the negatives, of taking away my passport. . . What then could I tell that little old lady who jumped out of a black luxury Mercedes sedan, refusing her chauffeur's help, and scurried across the Piazza di

Spagna like a mouse in order to rush up to me and yank my necktie like pulling the cord of a bell, her face up against mine: "Better to tie a rock around your neck and drown in the deepest sea than to create such a scandal against those people!"

With the help of her chauffeur I got her back to the car, making excuses, and in truth I felt a bit disturbed. Like that other time in Padua, at two o'clock on an August afternoon, when all alone I saw on a church door an enormous poster with a black border and the inscription: "Let us pray for the salvation of the soul of Federico Fellini, public sinner."

To confront the reality of our lives, to understand our historic moment is generally considered a moral obligation. Is it for you? What do you think of the world in which we live?

I don't rely on opinions; I reject them right away.

It has always seemed to me a hopeless task to set up political projections based on events and to diagnose them. I don't have the measuring instruments or the enthusiasm for it. I am aware that mine is a childish shortcoming, but I don't see myself having the maturity of thought, the objectivity, or the remarkable intuition necessary to understand what directs society and by what obscure labyrinths it has arrived at certain dead ends. I don't believe the world is directed by a dark, prophetic superbrain. I'm afraid it just drifts along. Perhaps there was a plan once which has since been forgotten, the same as happened to the Church's plan for the salvation of mankind. At the beginning there must have been a Word, but since then a built up network of safeguards and rituals has made us forget it. Only the labyrinth of rituals has remained, without our remembering the entrance and exit any more or even how to move within it. Maybe the way is just to move somehow, so as to transform our agony into nourishment for ourselves and for others. This accounts for the fascination of the novels of Kafka and Borges.

Those like me who don't have a scientific view of things, nor measure progress in rational terms, give themselves over to more or less pleasant dreams or dark guilt complexes which reveal through daily life, we believe, the radiance promised in the Apocalypse of St. John or in the prophesies of Nostradamus. The strongest temptation is to say that the future is already over. Maybe it's because I have read so much science fiction, but at times I too share in the foolish aggression, the monstrous egotism which catches up mankind during its destruction of the natural resources of the planet. The prospect is catastrophic, but I accept it from several points of view: because as a filmmaker I find it enticing, and because of the Catholic harassment we have borne for 2,000 years. Besides, to suggest a weak reason for why progress falls short, it seems to me that the whole business is a matter of selfish enthusiasm about getting on another Noah's ark and traveling through the center of the disaster with a chosen few and some animals.

But what do you think are your responsibilities?
The only responsibility I feel is to avoid "coming close," which is a direct result of stupidity and ignorance. To come close is a typically Italian way, a psychological attitude we have always cultivated and enjoy tending. We have even presumed at times that it is a resource, something in the genes that others envy. But almost always it is nothing but a sorry surrender, just to survive—coming close to surviving, that is. I feel a responsibility not to deceive, not to be simply content. I need to testify to the complexities I find by the rigorous application of that expressive instrument at my disposal. I must never just come close to exactitude: with color, with life, with the right scene at the right moment. And I must not forget that artistic expression also has a playful side while proposing a vision of things, while sharing with others a good or bad moment, while welcoming imagination into the game. At a

time laden with uncertainty and fear, to lift our eyes from the depths, from the practical, from the everyday can make us feel guilty of enjoying a luxury or a perversion. Instead of finding a sense of freedom, we are made to feel that even the use of free time must be an obligation. That way it becomes an empty time in no way related to one's self or with life. We have less and less room for aesthetic contemplation, understood in the Greek sense as a tendency to love beauty. Beauty would seem less deceitful and insidious if we began to consider beautiful everything that evokes feeling independent of established rules. However we reach it the emotional sphere releases energy, which is always positive, be it from an ethical or an aesthetic point of view. The beautiful is also good; intelligence is good; beauty is also intelligence: the one and the other liberate us from our cultural prison.

What else moves you profoundly?

Innocence. I immediately surrender to anyone innocent and judge myself severely: children, animals, the way certain dogs will look at you. The extreme modesty I sometimes see in the desires of humble people has the power to disturb me. And of course beauty moves me: the glances of certain charmingly beautiful ladies who seem to fill the air around them with a special light; poignant sights; creative expression: a writer or a painter who manages to capture on paper or on canvas a sense of the ways of the world, a vision that will last forever, touches me with profound emotion.

On the other hand nature leaves me indifferent, listless. I know, it's monstrous, it's pathological, and I can't manage to explain this shortcoming of mine. I don't really see nature and experience it, except as memories: the woods I saw as a child, the sea, nightfall. . . But a beautiful countryside today, a sunset, the primordial grandeur of the mountains, the silence of a snowfall, move me only if I can reproduce them at Cinecittà, in the theater, fusing them together with silk and gelatin.

What things are you most ashamed of?
The foolishness I utter during interviews; intimate conversation; my idle chatter even without being asked to speak; and the silences into which I fall when I ought to speak. I'm ashamed of being vague, pliable, imprudent.

Sometimes I'm also a little ashamed of not being sure of anything. Anyone who in an innocent disarming way claims to be unsure always makes me feel a little uneasy, embarrassed, uncertain, inconsistent. I am like a curious yet bored tourist, a passerby, someone who is and isn't there. A

143

person who can get passionately angry, who twists and turns, who swears convincingly, who hates and loves blindly, I eye with a mixture of stupor and admiration.

I don't remember where I read that the psychological type defined as "artistic" continually wavers between two feelings within him: shining exaltation, semi-divine satisfaction; and depression, guilt, blame, punishment. Those two contrasting modes of feeling are the opposite sides of an artist's life, experienced more or less consciously. At times he finds them a curse, at others an exceptionally gratifying state of being.

The Catholic Church with its profound knowledge of the human soul has justifiably treated artists as children: on the one hand stimulating their creativity with gifts and rewards, so that they would dedicate their talents to the glory of her saints, her martyrs, her myths; but at the same time relentlessly fostering the feeling of guilt that an artist must feel toward work that has no immediate use and a life lived outside the rules, preyed upon by dark powers that lead him to sin against the lawful, the legitimate, the commandments, the conventional order.

You spoke of gifts and awards made by the Church to artists. What place has money in your life?

I have a very hazy notion of the real value of money and therefore its relationship to the value of things. I happen, for example, to be totally indifferent to large figures (and therefore spend money senselessly); on the other hand I have ridiculous reactions to tiny sums of money, which I pay out with the hesitation and reluctance of someone who is being robbed. I think my unrealistic view of money has deep rooted feelings from episodes of my early youth when, barely arrived in Rome and during the war, making both ends meet became a dramatic experience. In that situation the value of money was greatly magnified: a thousand lire became peace, tranquillity, the Nobel Prize.

I went through a Bohemian period in the early days, but it was very brief: just enough so that in later stories I could romanticize it, inventing dinners of just coffee with cream and escapes from hotels by lowering my suitcase out the window. I earned money rather fast and with relative ease. I am not rich and I don't know how to do planning to become rich, because it doesn't interest me. I have no possessive feelings; it disturbs me to possess things; I don't like possessing anything. I get rid of pens, wristwatches—even a full wardrobe makes me want to throw it all out.

I don't play. I don't take vacations. I don't understand anything about boats, and even automobiles as I already said no longer appeal to me. I am not capable of possessing, collecting, storing. Luckily, within modest limits however, like most women my wife Giulietta likes to own things, which guarantees a somewhat generous lifestyle, though a bit more cautious than mine.

I have some ridiculously excessive stingy periods, suddenly debasing myself with senseless deprivations. For an entire month, for example, I took the bus: enough of twenty taxis a day, long live public transport! I don't know how this hunger for buses and trams seized me: whether from desire to return to a time when I was very young or a kind of unconscious wish to get back in with the people. Perhaps it was a need to reinvent a period by redoing the things that I did in 1937. Standing at a tram stop along with a housewife with her grocery sack must be a kind of reaction to old age moving relentlessly forward.

Let's have a brief detour before returning to films. What is your day like when you're not working? Are you a morning person? Do you get up early?

Yes, and with no need to be called. I have a mental clock which I can set in advance with only a few minutes margin for error, and in whatever bed I find myself. I wake up suddenly, immediately, like lighting a lamp. I have always slept very little, even when small. I try to recall fragments of the dream which in the night, lazy, half asleep, I forgot to write down, convinced I would remember it; but instead I don't.

Then I move about the empty silent house, opening doors, turning on lights, sitting in an armchair, a sofa, behind a table, like a crazy cat who wants to try out every spot. I hum, I yawn, I open and close a great number of drawers discovering a lot of things belonging to the house that I didn't know about or had forgotten about. Finally I open the windows, which seems to me the only useful thing I can do in a house, where my lack of manual dexterity is absolute. I have never turned on the gas; I am ignorant of what to do to light the flame. I'm ashamed to say it, but even turning on the television is always a bit of an adventure, and if I'm alone I let it be. In the bathroom I move back and forth in front of the mirror three or four times watching myself out of the corner of one eye. Then I decide to look at myself: new damages? New devastations? Ruins? And that look? Who could trust someone with a face like that?

Don't you even know how to cook an egg?
No, I have no patience for it. My job as director requires the patience of a saint. I can spend hour

after hour, sometimes entire afternoons, searching for just the right lighting arrangement; on the other hand I can't stand waiting even a few minutes for a cup of coffee to heat up.

Another contradiction: I know I have a certain manual ability; I design, I fool around with clay, I make models. On the set I like to busy myself with everything: I straighten pictures, arrange wigs, move furniture—in sum, I know how to use my hands rather well. In the kitchen I become a disaster, a character out of an old comic scene: broken plates, slips and falls, wounds, burns.

One time at Fregene I did some cooking, for some fifty cats who were meowing threateningly in the garden. It was winter and ours was the only villa still remaining open. I made a huge minestrone, emptying out the whole refrigerator, even adding in a bottle of Activarol, an energy tonic that I wasn't taking any more. The dish was a success.

It is now very stylish to talk about one's body. What about yours?

I instinctively tend to take care of it; moreover, thinking about it, I want to be healthy in order to work. Illness is an unforeseen obstacle which I'm afraid of, like tax notices, the cancellation of a flight, meeting a friend from school whom you don't remember at all but he remembers you.

148

"On the set I like to busy myself with everything."

I am frugal at the table, temperate, and don't give way to excesses. At least so it seems to me. But I have never done body building and I regret that because I would like to be powerful and challenge the strong who threaten the weak, like a character in a comic strip. Instead, from childhood I gave the impression of having minor illnesses—perhaps another Catholic heritage—in order to seem victimized, persecuted, and to complain about the injustices one suffers.

Do you go to beauty parlors?
Do you? Sometimes seeing the ravages of baldness, jaundice spots on the skin, wrinkles, growths, I think that one day or other I'll telephone my dear friend in Milan who has told me about a clinic in Russia where you enter at the age of seventy and don't get out until you're seventy-one, literally, because the therapy lasts one year. But you get out looking like a healthy sixty-nine year old. That is what my friend tells me, who is a little younger than I but has white hair and doesn't remember any more exactly where this clinic is.

Would you care to say precisely what you like and don't like?
A magazine—I think *L'Espresso*—a while ago had a similar quiz and they asked me. My list has generally remained the same.

I don't like: parties, festivals, tripe, interviews, round tables, requests for autographs, escargots, traveling, standing in line, mountains, ships, the radio turned on, music in restaurants, music in general (when I have to put up with it), wire broadcasting, jokes, soccer fans, the ballet, creches, gorgonzola, awards, oysters, hearing people talk about Brecht over and over, official dinners, toasts, speeches, being invited, requests for advice, Humphrey Bogart, quizzes, Magritte, being invited to art shows, theater rehearsals, stenotype machines, tea, camomile, caviar, the preview of anything, citations, he men, films for the young, theatricality, temperament, questions, Pirandello, crepes suzettes, beautiful countrysides, subscriptions, political films, psychological films, historical films, obligation and release from obligation, ketchup.

I like: the seasons, Matisse, airports, rice, oak trees, Rossini, roses, the Marx brothers, tigers, waiting for appointments and hoping that the other person won't come (even if it's a beautiful woman), Toto, not having been there, Piero della Francesca, everything beautiful about a beautiful woman, Homer, Joan Blondell, September, nougat ice cream, cherries, beautiful asses on bicycles, trains and boxed lunches on trains, Ariosto, cocker spaniels and dogs in general, the smell of wet earth, the smell of hay, bending laurels, cypress trees, the sea in winter, people who speak very little, James Bond, the one-step, empty places, deserted restaurants, squalor, empty churches, silence, Ostia, the sound of bells, finding myself alone in Urbino on Sunday afternoon, basel, Bologna, Venice, all of Italy, Raymond Chandler, women concierges, Simenon, Dickens, Kafka, Jack London, roast chestnuts, the subway, taking the bus, large high beds, Vienna (but I have never been there), waking up, going to sleep, postcard shops, Faber No. 2 pencils, vaudeville before a film, bitter chocolate, secrets, the dawn, night, spirits, Wimpy, Laurel and Hardy, Lana Turner, Leda Gloria—I also like Greta Gonda a great deal—soubrettes and also ballerinas.

Getting back to your films, we have arrived at The Temptation of Dr. Antonio, *an episode from* Boccaccio '70 *which you wrote as a satire on the censors of* La Dolce Vita. *It was your first film in color. Why color, and when do you prefer color to black and white?*

There is no rule for when color should be used instead of black and white or visa versa. In a rotten film color is always preferable to black and white. Especially when you think how much even bland or foolishly realistic use of color can stifle the imagination. The closer you get to miming reality the more you lapse into imitation. And black and

152

white offers too great a scope to the imagination in a situation like that.

When to choose color? When the film seems to need it; when your first images of it come in color; when color becomes a totally expressive material, becomes the story, structure, feeling of the film, becomes the means by which to translate, to narrate all of that: like in a dream where color is a concept, a feeling, the way it is in painting. The question so many ask: "Do you dream in black and white or in color?" is fatuous. It's like asking if there are sounds in singing, when everyone knows that sound is the means of expressing a song. When you dream you might see a red meadow, a green horse, a yellow sky. And these are not absurdities. They are images intrinsic to the feeling that inspires them.

The problem, if there is one, lies in the technique of translating color. In film images it isn't possible to define color with the same precision in all tonal nuances as one can, for example, in pictorial images which have the advantage of a fixed, steady, unchanging light. A contagion, literally, infects the colors of scene, a fluid interchange which makes for a continuous breaking of boundaries. I think though, aside from the sense of impotence that often grips you when you come up against that unforeseen contagion and makes you weep for your beautiful beloved black and white, color enriches a film with a new dimension, that of dream symbolism, a quality profoundly interlinked with film.

And light? What about light?

Light is the very substance of a film. In film—I have said this before—light is ideology, feeling, color, tone, profundity, atmosphere, storytelling. Light is what adds, cancels out, reduces, exalts, enriches, creates nuances, underlines, alludes to; it makes the fantastic and the dream believable and acceptable or, on the other hand, makes reality fantasy and turns everyday drabness into mirage; it adds transparency, suggests tensions and vibrations. Light excavates a face or smooths it out, creates expression where none exists, endows dullness with intelligence, makes the insipid seductive. Light outlines the elegance of a body, glorifies a countryside which may be nothing by itself, gives a background magic. Light is the premier special effect, a kind of makeup, a sleight of hand, an enchantment, an alchemist's shop, a mechanism for marvels. Light is the hallucinatory salt which, burning, unleashes visions. Whatever lives on film lives by means of light. The most elementary or crudely made set design can by means of light reveal unexpected perspectives or steep the story in a hushed, brooding atmosphere.

Satyricon. "Light...glorifies a countryside."

Juliet of the Spirits. "Light . . . makes the fantastic and the dream believable."

Or merely by replacing a powerful light source with shadows, change of light can dissolve a sense of agony and turn everything serene, familiar, reassuring. Films are written in light, their style expressed by means of light.

We have come to 8½ which many consider your finest film, widely imitated to the point of becoming a genre, like the western, the detective story, the historical film, science fiction, war films. In almost every country in the world there has been and probably will be again directors who will make or want to remake their own 8½.

I on the other hand didn't want to make it. The night before the shooting, desperate, confused, I wrote old Rizzoli, the producer, a letter which began: "Dear Angelino, I realize that what I am about to tell you will irreparably terminate our working relationship. Even our friendship will be jeopardized. I should have written this letter three months ago, but until last night I had hoped that. . ."

The troupe and many of the leading actors had already been hired; sets were being completed; in fact, from the office where I was writing I was listening to the carpenters' hammers. Why then did I want to back out, leave it all up in the air, get away? What had happened? Only this: I didn't

157

remember any more what the film was that I wanted to make. The feeling, the essence, the flavor, the silhouette, the flash of light that had seduced and fascinated me had disappeared, dissolved. I couldn't find them any more.

During the last weeks, with growing anxiety I tried to retrace the course of development of that film whose title I couldn't even decide on. In my appointments book I had written, provisionally, "8½" referring to the number of movies I had made. But how was the idea born? What was the first contact with, the first presentiment of, that film? A vague confused desire to create the portrait of a man on a certain day of his life. The portrait of a man, I told myself, with all his contradictory, nuanced, elusive totality of different realities. A portrait in which all the possibilities of his being happened—their levels, story after story, like in a building whose facade is crumbling, revealing its entire inside: stairways, corridors, rooms, lofts, cellars, and the furniture of every room, the doors, roofs, plumbing, the most intimate, most secret corners.

A life made up of tortuous, changing, fluid labyrinths of memory, of dreams, of feelings, of the everyday inextricably bound up with memories, imaginings, feelings, happenings that took place long ago and join with those occurring now; a mingling of nostalgia and presentiment in a serene yet mixed up time, where our character doesn't know who he is any more or who he was or where his life is going; a life that now seems only a long wakeful sleep, devoid of feeling.

I was speaking of this one evening with Flaiano while driving toward the sea at Ostia. Talking about it I tried to clarify for myself the intention of the film. Flaiano was quiet, didn't say a word, made no comment, seemed suspicious, defiant, jealous. I had the impression that he didn't think the theme belonged on film, that my narrative was a presumptuous, excessive, arrogant outpouring in a dimension that only literature could achieve. Tullio Pinelli, to whom I tried to communicate the sense of this fleeting fantasy a few days later, was also silent, perplexed, doubtful perhaps of the possibility of building a story on an impulse so whimsical and so difficult to translate into situations and events.

On the other hand Brunello Rondi, with his usual overflowing enthusiasm, went along with it. He is an invaluable audience; he likes everything, is excited by every project, is ready to go off and collaborate in all directions on anything. We began to write separately, the four of us. I would suggest theme, a conflict, a situation, and Pinelli, Flaiano and Brunello each would script his own version of the sequence.

However I had not yet decided what type of man we would try to portray, what his profession would be: a lawyer? an engineer? a journalist? One day I decided to put my dream hero in a spa. It then seemed to me that the intention of the film began to take on more solid possibilities. We wrote the harem sequence; the night in the baths with the hypnotist friend; the hero now had a wife and a mistress. But then the plot began to unravel altogether. It didn't have a central core from which to develop, nor a beginning, nor could I imagine how it might end. Every morning Pinelli asked me what our hero's profession was. I still didn't know, and it still didn't seem important to me, though I began to get a little nervous.

One day I decided it was useless to go on with the script. I felt that if I wanted to get on with the film I had to begin to look the characters in the eye, to select the actors, to determine the settings, to decide on an infinity of things; then go in search of my film among the people: in clothing shops, at Fiuggi or Montecatini, in theaters; then organize the troupe, talk to the decorator, to the projectionist; to pretend, in sum, that the film was ready and that we would begin shooting within a month. I decided on Mastroianni, chose Sandra Milo, had Anouk Aimeé come in from Paris, and in a forest near Rome began to construct the thermal palace, and in the Scalera production studios the grandmother's farm and the hotel rooms. The vast production mechanism was set in motion: dates, contracts, production plans, estimates, advances. But I, shut in my office, couldn't manage to find my film again: it wasn't there any more; it had gone away. I admitted that maybe it had never existed.

And here we are back to the tale of the letter I was writing to Rizzoli, an edifying tale straight from the heart. I was in the middle of that letter when I heard the booming voice of Menicuccio, the chief machinist, calling me from the courtyard to come to the theater for a moment because Gasparino (another machinist) was celebrating his birthday and offering glasses of champagne. He would be pleased if "the doctor" were there too.

And there I am in the theater. Carpenters, mechanics and painters were all waiting for me, all of them with glasses in their hands, in the huge kitchen under construction; it duplicated the one in my grandmother's country house, but enlarged by my memory of it. Gasparino, a bricklayer's cap on his head and a hammer strapped to his thigh, opened the bottle: "This will be a great film, doctor. Your health! Long live *8½*!" The glasses were emptied, everybody applauded, and I felt overwhelmed by shame. I felt myself the least of men, the captain who abandons his crew. I didn't go back up to the office where my half-written copout letter was waiting for me, but instead sat down, blank and emptied, on a little bench in the garden in the middle of a great coming and going of workers, technicians, actors belonging to other working troupes. I told myself I was in a no exit situation. I was a director who wanted to make a film he no longer remembers. And lo and behold, at that very moment everything fell into place. I got straight to the heart of the film. I would narrate everything that had been happening to me. I would make a film telling the story of a director who no longer knows what film he wanted to make.

Yes, but in the "story of a director who no longer knows what film he wanted to make," other elements also enter in with a new clarity, such as dreams and the very language of dreams. How did these elements which essentially characterize the film come about?

The reading of several books by Jung, the discovery of his vision of life, took on for me the nature of a joyous revelation, an enthusiastic, unexpected, extraordinary confirmation of something that I myself seem to have foreseen to some small extent. I owe this providential, stimulating, fascinating discovery to a German psychotherapist named Bernhard. I don't know whether Jungian thought has influenced my films

8½

from *8½* on. I only know that reading several of his books has undoubtedly helped and encouraged my contact with more profound and stimulating areas of the imagination. I have always thought I had one major shortcoming: that of not having general ideas about anything. The ability to organize my likes, tastes, desires in terms of genre or category has always been beyond me. But reading Jung I feel freed and liberated from the sense of guilt and the inferiority complex that the shortcoming I touched upon always gave me.

Do you think that psychoanalysis, helping man to know himself better, has always made him happier?

I don't know how to answer that question because I don't know how to define happiness. I think that psychoanalysis should be studied in the schools, is a science that should be taught even before the others. Because it seems to me that among life's many adventures, the one most worth the hassle of taking on is that voyage which plunges you into your interior dimensions so as to explore the unknown part of your self. And notwithstanding all the risks it offers, what other adventure could be as fascinating, marvelous, and heroic?

Yours seems to me a rigidly Jungian view. Don't you think you're denying Freud's role its proper setting?

I am not entirely able to give you a scientific or critical response to two thinkers of such stature and complexity who have brought to life fundamental aspects of the human soul which now penetrate our culture. We are participants in and recipients of their thought, beyond measure.

I have read less Freud and can only express guarded, uncertain impressions. Perhaps Freud is a more gifted writer than Jung on a literary level. But his strictness, while it enlists my admiration, makes me uneasy. He is a teacher who overwhelms me with his competence and certainty. Jung is a traveling companion, an older brother, a sage, a seer-scientist who, it seems to me, is less proud of himself and his marvelous discoveries. Freud wants to explain to us what we are; Jung accompanies us to the door of the unknowable and lets us see and understand by ourselves.

Jung's scientific humility in confronting the mystery of life seems more likeable to me. His thoughts and ideas don't pretend to be doctrine, only suggest a new point of view, a different attitude which can enrich and evolve our personality. They guide us toward a more aware, more open way of life and reconcile us with the remote, frustrated, mortified, sick parts of our selves. Jung is undoubtedly more congenial, more friendly, more nourishing for someone who believes he needs to

find himself in the dimension of creative imagination. Freud with his theories makes us think;
Jung on the other hand allows us to imagine, to
dream and to move forward into the dark labyrinth
of our being, to perceive its vigilant, protective
presence.

From the little I have read one thing more than
the others has impressed me: the different views
Freud and Jung have of the phenomenon of
symbolism. The problem has interested me, since
as a movie director I am led to use symbolic images
in my work. For Jung a symbol expresses an
intuition better than any other expression of it. For
Freud a symbol substitutes for something else
which should be done away with and therefore is
better forgotten than expressed. For Jung, then,
a symbol is a way of expressing the inexpressible,
albeit ambiguously. For Freud it is a way of hiding
what is forbidden to express.

It seems to me that this area clearly shows the
different approaches to being of the two great
thinkers. It is a matter, I repeat, of two different
ways of delineating the human soul. That of Jung
seems more fascinating to me.

Between Juliet of the Spirits *and* Toby Dammit,
your episode in Spirits of the Dead, *there is a three
year break. In* Toby Dammit *I seem to hear an almost*

funereal knell. You were very ill and thinking about The Voyage of Mastorna.

Who knows who this gentleman is in the Milan phone book which I opened at random to look for a name for the hero of some story I had in mind to make, which up to that time was called only *The Voyage*?! Dino Buzzati, who was great at coming up with strange and at the same time real sounding names, was proposing some twenty of them. Each time before telling me one he would utter an amused, slightly evil giggle. "Encircle," he giggled, "engineer Ermete Squoiato, with an 0!" he suggested. "Rondò, Tullio Rondò. Scidmeno. No, better Scimno, Paolo Scimno." I much enjoyed listening to him, but after half an hour I asked for the phone book. And out came Mastorna.

I have talked about this film so much. Punctually two or three times a year a journalist friend asks me for news about its health, asks if this is its turn, and if I'll finally make that beloved *Mastorna.* In good faith I tell him yes; and at the end of each film its beguiling ghost appears and asks to be brought to life. And each time something happens to submerge it again, a glorious bit of flotsam in the profound depths where it has lain now for some twenty years. And from there it continues to send out prodigious fluids, radioactive currents that have nourished all the films I have made in its place.

I am certain that without *Mastorna* I would not have imagined *Satyricon,* or at least I would not have imagined it the way I made it; nor *Casanova,* nor the *City of Women.* Even *The Ship Sails On* and *Orchestra Rehearsal* owe a small debt to *Mastorna.* The strange thing is that the story, even though it generously nourished so many of my other films, remains miraculously intact in its narrative structure. It has not lost dimension or substance and remains always the most real of all of the stories I have been able to imagine. I don't know how to explain the strange destiny of this film. Perhaps it's not a film at all but an admonition, a stimulus, a story guide; perhaps it serves the same function as those tugboat operators who pull transatlantic liners out of port: something, in sum, born not to be made but to permit others to be made. A kind of inexhaustible creative uranium.

Once in the waiting room of the Copenhagen airport I saw a metal suitcase with its corners somewhat dented. Someone had left it near me on the floor. On the identification card beside the handle was written "Mastorna," "J. Mastorna." I looked around for the owner, but the loudspeaker was announcing the departure of my flight. And even had I been tempted to stay there to see the face of this mysterious traveler, I found myself pulled toward the exit by the passengers embarking. The suitcase remained there all alone, abandoned on the floor of the waiting room which was now deserted, and then slowly began filling up with new travelers. Only at the last moment, when I was already on the bus carrying me to the plane I seemed to see through the window someone bending over to pick up the suitcase. It was a woman. A black woman. Bah! More and more improbable, this *Mastorna*.

Wouldn't you want to give us a hint at this time as to what The Voyage of Mastorna *is about?*

I won't even try. I can tell you that whenever somebody asks me for information about a film I'm about to make, an unconscious fear rises up that swiftly hides the film the way a smoke screen changes, deforms, conceals for protection. So that I tell a different story to my journalist friends about a different film. Perhaps it's an aggressive form of modesty or jealousy. I fear for the life of that project lying naked and defenseless in a vulnerable area. And to discuss it seems to me to betray it or, worse, to risk altering its hypothetical indefinable form. I also have the embarrassed feeling that talking about a film before making it is indiscreet, like those arrogant and ungracious braggarts who gossip about a married woman they scarcely know. What's the good of this badmouthing? What's the good of anticipating something which, when finished, will probably turn out very different from the way it was conceived.

If finally, out of courtesy, fatigue, friendship or vanity I should begin to chat about *Mastorna* I doubt I could manage to convey the meaning of a film which, in the first place, I myself don't know. I could say one more time that it is a journey, imagined or dreamed, a journey into memory, into repression, into a labyrinth that has an infinity of exits but only one entrance, and that therefore the real problem is not to get out but to get in. And I could go on blatantly rattling off definitions and proverbs. *Mastorna* is the hint of a film, the shadow of a film, perhaps even a film that I don't know how to make.

Let's leave Mastorna *then and talk of another voyage, into the pagan world of Petronius*, Satyricon.

Satyricon was, along with *Casanova, The Decameron* and *Orlando Furioso* one of the films I promised the producers to make ever since the time of *I Vitelloni*, a goodie in exchange for a film like *La Strada* or whatever else really interested me. I never really expected to keep those promises. However during my convalescence from allergic pleurisy I reread Petronius and was fascinated by an element I had not noticed before: the missing

parts; that is, the blanks between one episode and
the next. Back in school when we studied the pre-
Pindaric poets I tried to imagine filling in the blanks
between their various fragments. Our teacher was
absolutely ridiculous in expecting sixteen year old
dummies to be enthusiastic when he declaimed in
his tiny voice the sole remaining verse of some
poet: "I drank leaning on my long spear." And I
was the source of great hilarity, inventing a whole
series of fragments which we were going to propose
to him, shameless as we were.

But that business of fragments really fascinated
me. I was struck by the idea that the dust of
centuries had conserved the beating of hearts
forever still. While I was convalescing at Manziana
I came across Petronius in the little library of the
pensione where I was staying. And again I felt a
strong emotion. It conjured up marble columns,
heads with missing eyes or shattered noses, the
graveyard aspect of the Appian Way, archaeological
museums: sparse fragments, in large part repressed
and forgotten, made whole by what might be called
a dream. Not by a historical epic reconstructed
philologically from documents and positively
verified, but by a great dream galaxy sunken in the
darkness and now rising up to us amid glowing
bursts of light. I think I was seduced by the
possibility of reconstructing this dream with its

puzzling transparency, its unreadable clarity. The same thing happens with real dreams. They have substance through which we express ourselves profoundly, but in the light of day our only conscious connection with them is as intellectual concepts. Therefore dreams appear to our conscious minds as fleeting, incomprehensible and alien. The ancient world, I told myself, never existed, but no doubt we dreamed it. My job will be to eliminate the borderline between dream and imagination; to invent everything and then to objectify the fantasy; to get some distance from it in order to explore it as something all of a piece and unknowable.

What do you remember of its impact on the public?
The premiere of *Satyricon* took place at Madison Square Garden right after a rock concert. There were 10,000 young people there. You could smell the heroin and hashish through the cigarette smoke. That fabulous army of hippies made a stupendous spectacle arriving on incredible motorcycles and in multicolored automobiles all lit up with lamps. It was snowing and the skyscrapers of Manhattan were all illuminated, huge slabs of glistening ice.

The show was a knockout. The young people applauded every scene; many slept, others made love. Amid total chaos the film went on relentlessly

Satyricon

on a giant screen that seemed to reflect an image of what was happening in the hall. Unpredictably, mysteriously, in that most improbable ambience *Satyricon* seemed to have found its natural site. It didn't seem mine any more in that sudden revelation of secrets understood, of subtle, unbroken links between the ancient Rome of memory and that fantastic audience from the future.

How do young people regard you?

I don't know them. I don't know where they are or what they are doing. I could surely try to find out all that, but isn't a task of that kind rather chilling? I ask myself what could have happened at a certain point in time, what kind of evil could have struck down our generation so that we suddenly looked upon youth as the harbingers of some kind of absolute truth. The young, the young, the young...they seem to have arrived on spaceships...they know everything, they tell us nothing, they don't want to be bothered with our ignorance, our errors...

It must have been a desire to see things begin again from the beginning and an awareness of having been defeated by our own lack of confidence that drove us, shockingly, to turn over all the keys to kids who don't know how to use them at all. It is fascinating and terrible to think how much

175

happened between 1950 and 1970 to make wiser generations hand over their power to one which has barely stopped playing with toys. Only a collective insanity could have made us consider fifteen year old kids our masters, the source of all truth. Maybe it's because we were tired of false masters who, confronting the destruction of everything we believed in, made it seem as though we shouldn't try to say anything any more...

Terrorism: do you think to some degree it could be a consequence, a sequel to all of that?

I don't have an answer for that either. But the situation doesn't seem that simplistic to me. Terrorism is a reality I have tried to understand. How can a young person shoot somebody in the head whom he doesn't know and think he can live with that crime all his life? What sickness has come over him? It may be that we have become too easily accustomed to thinking—even our favorite poets do—that war justifies murder. But when there is no war all this seems infinitely more savage and untenable. I can, although with effort, comprehend shooting someone we consider an enemy, but I find it difficult to imagine how we can eliminate a sense of guilt.

Hitler, Stalin, the great tyrants, had the power of a collective unconscious incarnate in themselves.

They became the center of dark desires, expressed a collective insanity. But for the hit man, the worker, to agree to murder uninspired by any ideal, his feeble mind, his primitive feelings in darkness? It makes you believe that in certain corners of the psyche we still retain the monstrous features of man the animal. I have no respect for those who, in the name of historical perspective, tell us we should refrain from condemning terrorism because it may be that certain crimes will be considered patriotic acts in the future. I don't have that kind of historical sense at all; it's a perspective that doesn't concern me. I am concerned with day to day living, with how much I can do while I am alive. All the rest seems like mere speculation to me.

How have you lived through our Italian "years of lead?" I'm not asking for an analysis of terrorism, rather how you lived through those events, how they influenced you?

I have always gone on working and work is a great protective screen, a suit of asbestos armor, even though hiding behind work seems a kind of cowardice or flight confronted with such abnormal events.

My feeling is that of impotence: a paralyzing feeling of not being able to do anything, as if your inner life has been horribly altered by a dark,

177

absurd, irrational guilt. It seems to have set something unavoidable in motion, as if we have all committed some dark unknown crime which unleashes an equally unknown destructive process, like a cancer, like a body struck by cancer. But where, how, when did we go so far wrong that we must give in with no hope of escape to so terrible a consequence. And also there is the fear that comes from seeing the State impotent, the police, the forces of law and order defeated. And there is the frightening, absurd surrender by the newspapers and by television news commentaries; and the funeral rites and the unbearable litany of denunciations by ministers of state.

A nightmare. Aggravated by the blurred vision of some commentators and newspapers who find justifications for it; by some imbecilic friends who somehow feel comforted by these persecutors of their neuroses and talk about them with sympathy, with ill concealed empathy; by some honorable men who call these butchers "confused comrades," "comrade assassins." And those stony faces, those beards, mustaches, Balaclava helmets. And psychoanalysts' patter in the weeklies: "They're trying to kill the emptiness inside them." "They're shooting at their own terror in order to destroy it." Or the even more strident analyses of sociologists and political scientists ready to accept this phenomenon as a fatality, an inevitable evolution.

The atrocities they have perpetrated: their ferocity toward those poor eighteen year old policemen, machine gunned at dawn in a foggy suburb while drinking coffee—on top of that the horrible pictures of those murders on the television, those pathetic corpses riddled with bullets looking like beef in a slaughter house. But perhaps even more than the atrocities, the most frightening thing is the abject cowardly "understanding" by so many intellectuals; their echoing of the senseless new jargon with its hateful phrases: "to kneecap," "up with the shooting." The flood of news on the front pages of the papers; the breathless pursuit, like a horrible treasure hunt, to find manifestos and messages in garbage cans; the newspaper columnists trembling with excitement taking down the language of death of those assassins.

The only consolation was the faces of the people at the funerals. The silence of those people rose up like a solid front against that insanity that wants to take over and infect everything.

I oppose with my own reason all possible historical or philosophical reasons—those are always too general and casually impersonal. My reason is based on the fact of abhorring violence in all its forms, manifestations, ideologies. I believe a person with an artistic bent is naturally conservative and needs order around him. Those people's shouts, songs, funeral corteges, shootings, barricades are disgusting and disturbing and make me want to shut them out. I don't have a revolutionary temperament and I doubt I ever had revolutionary friends. Noisy rebellion has no respect for the peace of others and is completely foreign to me. I need order because I am a transgressor; I even recognize myself as one. And to carry out my transgressions I need very strict order, with many taboos, obstacles at every step, moralizing, processions, alpine choruses filing along. That way I can be decorated by constituted authority, by the mayor, by the cardinal, as a transgressor to whom honor is paid.

Let us now take stock. Are you pleased with the way you've used your imagination these years? Do you think it has quickened our pace of life, made things clearer, made existence more bearable?

I have the mortifying suspicion that whenever I signed a contract to make a film I never once thought that I was bound to quicken our pace of life, make things clearer, make existence more bearable. Is that bad? I make films because I don't know how to do anything else. At least that's how it seems to me.

This interview will appear some thirty years after your first directorial effort. Make a kind of balance sheet: regrets, remorse, hopes?

I have no regrets. Those that I do have do not call for confession here. I have made the films I wanted to make and in the way I knew they should be made. I would rather not put my name to them from here on out, because I'm certain that without that ridiculous and paralyzing sense of responsibility-by-name I would make them better, with greater freedom, greater ease, as a pleasant carefree game. I would have liked to have been born twenty years earlier and made films with the pioneers, with Za-la-Mort, Za-la-Vie and Polidor, in that traveling-players atmosphere with the setting sun as a curtain. To participate in the birth of the movies would have been much more gratifying to my temperament than to arrive when specific film rules were imposed: structuralism, semiology. Inevitable things which keep you posted on artistic and cultural conditions but deprive you of that uproarious and disquieting atmosphere, that somewhat savage joy that linked the cinema to the circus and made it feel like a symbolic essence of life's intrigues. I regret having lost too much time between films and having let some continue and others disappear, but I disown nothing. It seems to me that given my bent—laziness, haphazardness, ignorance and a tendency to flounce around—things have gone very well. How could I have hoped for so much?

My personal life has also been fortunate. I have been quite protected, and perhaps I have helped to make it go well by allowing myself to be led: when situations drive me, invite me, beckon to me, I have never offered any resistance. If the general tendency of my life has been the need to tell stories through images, it seems to me that my private life has been organized in such a way that my work has become its most important part. My wife, friends, affections or absence thereof. . . I can state that there have been no distractions, no responsibilities, no pricks of conscience that have taken time away from my work.

If on the other hand my life had gone otherwise and yet I still went on making films, then the ledger sheet might be more embarrassing. But the certainty is that I would never have changed the way I work. I have made visual images profound; I have freed myself from schemes set up by others. But the universe in which I live has remained the same. With the passing of years I have lived at various levels, but no one more profound or ampler than the others. As a child I saw enchanted things under the circus tent. Now I own the works. I shape it and I move it. I arrived a guest in the hotel.

Now I am its owner. I can be the porter and the bellboy but also the maharajah who takes the suite on the first floor. Hopes? I don't have many illusions and so have no need to project into the future. And if there are empty spaces to fill up, I can do what has to be done. I am not particularly dedicated to my friends, to others, even to my wife. Yet I would still have more than enough to choose from.

There are those who say that now you live off your legend and do little to renew your inventive capacity. Truthfully, with the advancing years do you perceive a decline in inspiration?

I don't know what my legend is, and as for my decline in inspiration it seems to me that my bad luck, or good luck, is that I don't perceive it. I don't perceive a diminished desire to do things—if that's what you mean—or even a slower rate of ideas or stimuli. These seem to me to go on at the same rate as before when I was chronologically younger. What I perceive the lack of more and more, as I have already said, is a programmer, someone who will schedule my work. Someone who will say, "Good, I understand: although you're over sixty you still enjoy making little theatricals. I'll see to it and relieve you of the crap. What would you like to make? *The Three Musketeers?* Good, make *The Three Musketeers. The Mysterious Island?* All of Poe?

The novels of Chandler? Are you going to do *Mastorna*, yes or no?" Look, I don't want to become rich. All I need is a monthly stipend and someone to organize my work. If I could find him I wouldn't have the slightest feeling of being depleted. If I were allowed to make such personal films, a sort of delightful masturbation all my own, I'd jump for joy to have to bring out a film on *The Count of Monte Christo* or some other popular nineteenth century novel.

Moving from one thing to another, do you think the Italian style of comedy is the kind best suited to our cinema?

Italian style comedy has depicted a particular moment in our society. Now after some time we have come to see in it a critical perception that it probably didn't have. It stimulates our curiosity or entertains us, the way turning the pages of an old photograph album would, where we discover things to laugh at. We are used to laughing at ridiculous fashions, find them funny or awkward or pathetic. But the old photograph never suspected it was evoking all of that; it confined itself to showing us just as we were.

It seems to me that Italian style comedy falls more under the category of coincidence. Its presentations were wholly satisfying in themselves, with its winks of an eye in search of sympathy. So that the whole critical apparatus which finds indignation and protest in it is fatally flawed. In Italian style comedy you feel that everyone is delighted: producer, script writer, director, actors, and naturally the public also. The people in the audience are mirrored in the film, the film in the audience; thus a game of identification goes on infinitely in reflections more and more blurred and intentions less and less recognizable. It seems to me that floating above all that is a somewhat disreputable joy, like the strident laughter of freed slaves, like obscene freedom of speech that offends officials merely to sanction its own triumph and reward its own self-indulgence. I don't like to seem ungenerous in speaking of films which, for the most part, I haven't seen and which should never be grouped together in a random genre, but instead should be considered individually. I realize that denouncing them doesn't mean much to those who watch stories that constantly build solidarity and self satisfaction, plus a fundamental misunderstanding, which is to consider ourselves better than the representation of the worst part of ourselves. It is certainly true that to evoke all of this they had to use excellent comic actors with real insights into our national characteristics, vices, defects, virtues, tics, physical traits—authentic comic talents, enthusiastic mimes relaxed and at home in this domain. But who can say whether they would not have found their niche along other roads, in other contexts?

There are those who say nastily that the Italian style of comedy mirrors certain aspects of our reality, and that you on the other hand distort it...

I don't think I distort reality at all. Essentially I portray it. To portray it I use one category, expression, to eliminate, choose, select, and regroup in order to achieve an equilibrium which is the story, the narrative. I require the public to participate in it, in my point of view, in my feeling. In that sense expression can be mistaken for distortion. Perhaps it is, being a filtered reality reorganized for representation. Reality is also warped by poetry, by painting—even the most naturalistic painting—by music. It is art as order, as harmony restructured from indifference and chaos, which leads to that inner understanding we define as aesthetic feeling. Therefore I never know what they mean about "my need to distort reality." It is a commonplace which I find pinned to my back and which often causes people to ask me with dazed admiration, but also with an air of seeming reproach: "But where do you find all those types?" A question without answer, since I don't look for and don't find those types. I simply see them. It seems to me sufficient to look at one's self in the mirror to perceive we are surrounded by comic, frightening, deformed, ugly, bewildered faces. Our faces, the faces of life.

You have always had many collaborators around you, often famous important ones. Is any one of them more valuable, more special than any of the others?

Indeed, I have had collaborators not only valuable for their talent, imagination and intelligence but also for the feeling of friendship I have when we work together; it takes on the joy and excitement of a visit to the country, a voyage, an excursion. I want to acknowledge some of them: Piero Gherardi, the set designer of *La Dolce Vita* and *Juliet of the Spirits*, aristocratic hobo, an intellectual guest in the house of Trimalchio (the vulgar wealthy boor of *Satyricon*), as wise and detached as a bonze and as greedy, gluttonous and immature as a newborn babe. I remember certain nights when we slept together in an automobile lost in a bandits' ravine. We were looking for a setting for the Country of Toys—I never admitted it, but *Pinocchio* was also among my uncompleted projects.

Another very close and congenial collaborator was Danilo Donati, a richly ingenious inventor of costumes and props. From the visual point of view

187

I consider *Satyricon* and *Casanova* among my most attractive films.

For a filmmaker the most important collaborators include not only set designers, cameramen and script writers but also a slick, canny, vigorous, unscrupulous production director. He can become the mainspring of the film.

Tullio Pinelli, with whom I have written so many sequences, I respect as an inventor of plots, a dramatic craftsman with regard to scenes and characters someone who has the calling and temperament of a true novelist. Including Ennio Flaiano, the equilibrium among us three seemed perfect to me. Pinelli concerned himself with narrative structure, that was his peg; and Flaiano did everything he could to demolish it, to break it into bits: at times he was more disastrous than a wild boar in a field of fava beans. But just because of these absolutely opposite tendencies, those parts of the walls that remained standing among the debris could be counted on to carry the structure of the narrative. Flaiano and I shared the same sense of humor about everything: a tendency to play it cool, kidding around, buffoonery, plus a touch of neurotic melancholy that makes me feel very close to him.

My encounters with Bernardino Zapponi have been stimulating. We have worked well together and share the same experiences and the same adventures: *Marc'Aurelio*, vaudeville curtain raisers; the same loves and enthusiasms: Poe, Dickens, Lovecraft, the occult, the spectral, mythological adventures, science fiction, and a bureaucratic feel for work that lies somewhere between its being unreal and fear of getting fired.

With Tonino Guerra I wrote *Amarcord* and *The Ship Sails On*. We share the same Italian dialect, an infancy spent among the same hills, snow, sea, and the San Marino mountain. The regions where we were born are nine kilometers apart. As a child I went by bicycle with other friends to his Sant'Arcangelo, and it seemed to us that they were speaking another language. In Rimini we looked upon Sant'Arcangelo as a colonial possession where the missionaries had not yet arrived: "Boss, the bearers want to turn back!" Titta would say, referring to the crude and inhospitable condition of Sant'Arcangelo.

But the most valuable collaborator of all, I can say without a second thought, was composer Nino Rota. Between us there was complete and total understanding, beginning with *The White Sheik*, the first film we made together. Our understanding had no need of adjustments on either part. I had decided to become a director and Nino was already at hand as if set in place so that I might continue

189

to do so. He had a geometric imagination and a musical vision worthy of the heavenly spheres, so that he didn't even have to see what my films looked like. When I would ask him what themes he had in mind for this or that sequence, it was immediately clear that no preview was necessary. His was an inner world where reality could scarcely penetrate. He lived music with the freedom and ease of someone in a dimension that is effortlessly his own.

He was a being possessed of a rare quality, a precious quality belonging to the realm of intuition. It was this gift that kept him so innocent and lovable and happy. But don't misunderstand me. When the occasion arose, or even when it didn't, he could say profound and perceptive things, could make impressively penetrating judgments about ideas and men. Like children, like simple souls, like certain sensitives, like certain innocent and guileless people he could suddenly utter brilliant remarks. . .

During work on my films I have the habit of using certain records as background noise: music can condition a scene, give it a rhythm, help suggest a solution, a character's attitude. There are themes that I have brought with me shamefully across the years, *La Titina, The March of the Gladiators*, tunes tied to specific emotions, to gut topics. Then obviously what happens when I have finished shooting the film is that I've grown fond of that improvised soundtrack and don't want to change it. Nino would agree with me right away, say that the themes I used during the shooting were absolutely beautiful (even though they were the most sugary and banal tunes); that they were just the right stuff and that he could never have been able to do better. And while he was saying that his fingers would caress the piano keyboard. "What was that?" I would ask a little later, "What were you playing?" "When?" Nino would ask in a distracted manner. "Now—I would insist—while I was talking you were playing something." "Ah, yes?—Nino would say—I don't know, I don't remember any more." And he would smile as though wanting to calm me down; I needn't have regrets or qualms; the records I used were more beautiful. And in the meantime he would continue to caress the keyboard as if by accident.

That is the way the captivating themes for my new films were born, making me forget my suggestions about the old tunes used during the shooting. I would stand there near the piano and talk to him about the film, explaining what I wanted to imply with this or that image, with this or that sequence. But he paid no attention to me, seemed to be thinking of something else while acquiescing or while nodding vigorous agreement. In reality he was establishing contact with his inner self, with the musical themes already within him. And when that contact was established he paid no attention to me any more, didn't listen to me any more. He put his hands on the piano and was transported like a medium, like a true artist. Finally I would say: "It is absolutely beautiful!" But he would answer: "I no longer remember." There might be catastrophies with tape recorders, with sound systems; those would have to be fixed without his knowing it. Otherwise his contact with the heavenly spheres would be broken...

It was a real joy to work with him. His creativity made me feel so close to it that it inspired a kind of giddiness, giving me the feeling that I myself was creating the music.

Nino would arrive at the end of the shooting, when the stress of retakes, montage, dubbing was at its peak. But as soon as he arrived the stress disappeared and everything turned into holiday. The film would enter a happy, serene fantasy world, an atmosphere which took on the quality of a new life. And it was always a surprise to me that after he had contributed so much feeling, so much emotion, so much life to the film that he would turn and point to the principal actor and ask: "Who is he?" "He's the leading man." I would answer. "What does he do—adding in a reproachful tone—you never told me anything about him!" Ours was a friendship nourished by sound.

I prefer not to hear music outside of my work. It conditions me, makes me nervous; I become possessed by it. I protect myself by rejecting it, by running away like a thief from temptation. Perhaps that too is Catholic conditioning: the fact that music makes me melancholy, burdens me with remorse, and with a stern voice tortures me by reminding me of a dimension of harmony, of peace, of completeness from which I am excluded, exiled. Music is cruel. It fills me with nostalgia and regret, and when it is ended I don't know where it has gone. I know only that the place is unattainable, and that makes me sad.

I can't even listen to someone tapping his fingers on the table without suddenly being disturbed and sucked in to the point where I breathe differently, in keeping with the rhythm. Nino, on the other hand, smack in the middle of a band noisily playing one of his themes, manages to write the notes of another theme which only he was listening to. A feat of magic that bowls me over!

How is it you have never directed an opera by Nino Rota? Do you have the same reservations about opera as about music in general?

Opera has an insane aspect that is truly fascinating. My reservations? That I don't know anything about it. That is, I know that opera is a part of my Italianate nature, like sharpshooters, Garibaldi, the Roman emperors. *Celeste Aida, Questa o quella per me pari sono, Stride la vampa* are arias that have been with me forever. I have always heard them. I have seen all my aunts, all my cousins weeping over their embroideries while they sang *Mi chiamano Mimi* and my grandfathers turn into savage beasts singing *"Se quel guerrier io fossi."* These things are so much ours that, like the unconscious, they turn into strangers. I feel an outsider's familiarity toward opera, the same as I feel about school, about vacation colonies, about all things that belong to a particular caste or that have a ceremonial quality: such things have always left me feeling alien and alone.

In my youth there was no one who didn't sing one of those mysterious phrases from an opera at some time: the ironsmith who came to repair the boiler sang; the mattress maker who stuffed those soft mattresses went about the house singing; and the domestic servants and those fabled apparitions, the knife grinder, the street sweeper. And if I would ask one of them, "Why do you say 'If I were that warrior?'" They would answer that it was from an opera and would begin to tell me the plot. And those plots were always gloomy, horrible, about savage vengeance, about lovers abandoned to a living death within a tomb.

Then there were the drunks who sang *Vecchia zimarra*—I have always slightly confused opera with drunks—at night, alone in the Piazza, their jackets fallen to the ground, they would sing all the operas at the top of their voices. Those were my first opera singers, the drunks.

When I was a child our house in Rimini was the last one on San Giuliano Street. Right beyond was the country road that led to Cesena. At Rimini we had the Vittorio Emanuele Theater, but I don't remember it well because it was usually closed for repairs. Since something was always broken there, opera was presented at the Bonci Theater in Cesena. And since the posters were put up in Rimini too, more than half the population, in carriages, in cars, by local train, went to Cesena to hear opera.

At four in the morning I would hear the wine-laden voices returning from Cesena, singing duets, choruses, arias. Seeing that slovenly troupe on bicycles, on foot, in carriages, in carts returning from Cesena when it was still dark, I imagined an invading army after who knew what raid. One morning, as daylight slowly came, in that vague clarity a certain Ubaldini, mad about music, stopped under our window and told me: "Call your mom and dad." He had heard *Andrea Chenier*, and with a most beautiful voice he began to sing *"Un di m'era di gioia. . ."* while the rabble filed on behind him.

Then he got sick because of the wine he had drunk. He was dragged into our house and set down on a rocking chair where, seemingly dead, he made quite an impression. However, after a bit he began singing again in a tiny voice, with his eyes still closed.

I have always felt like an outsider carrying a vague sense of guilt because of not wanting to participate in this warm, enveloping, impassioned, collective Italian ritual. Why couldn't I accept my dark Italianate side, this profound and subtly obscene ritual enclosing us all like in an amniotic sac? For it seems to me that opera—with its stunning effects, its law-breaking aspects, entombments, vendettas, love extending from here to the limits of imagination, pathological aspects—accurately expresses what's happening, even by the mistakes it makes. Opera doesn't exist separately from what is going on. For so many years it has coexisted alongside the unity of Italy, war, Fascism, the Resistance. How to go about restoring its original purity? Opera is a ritual, a Mass, a shepherd's song. Yet the present product must be respected for what it has done even in the different lifestyles of regional Italy. Why try to bring rigor of expression to a form that instead draws its vitality from the fact that it is just right as it is, like something happening fresh that evening, like a procession or a funeral?

I don't think it's fear of failure; I don't have those fears! But I would turn out a false product. It is respect for my own work that holds me back, that makes me incapable. I am too ignorant of the opera stage. I would be treated like someone who, no matter what he asks for, would have to be satisfied with what he gets. Also, they would have to be telling me what to do. If at least I had revolutionary ideas about opera! Instead, I believe it gets along quite well as it is, exactly as it is.

One evening on TV I saw a frenzied adaptation of *La Traviata*. The director and the cameramen went back and forth across the stage like expectant fathers in a maternity ward. Cameras zooming in on everything: on the rugs, on shoes, on the nails in the planks, on the singers' gold fillings. They might as well have added a shot of some detergent. The first shots that came on the screen showed us that the tenor was from Caserta and the soprano from Venice.

Well, in spite of that butchered adaptation, in spite of the faces of the singers, and although I was sitting alone in a little lamplit room in my home hearing from time to time the howlings of police cars in the street hurrying who knows where—in spite of all that I wept the entire evening. The first act ended and I wept. The second act began and right away, by the third note, I began weeping again, delighted to be doing so.

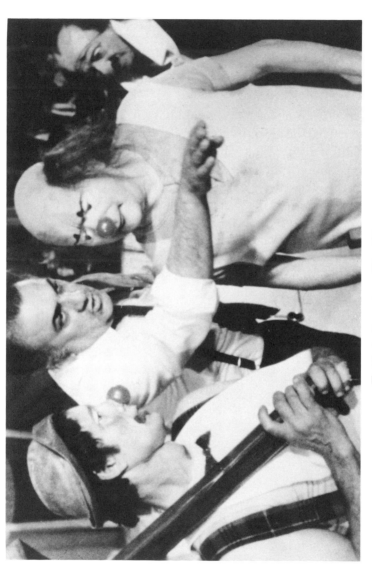

Fellini directing *The Clowns*

Perhaps that opera, *La Traviata*, is absolute perfection, a sphere of pure sentiment. Even the looney on the TV could not manage to destroy it. Well, if that's the case, who could do more with it than Verdi has done?

The Clowns, Roma, Amarcord...*the beginning of the 1970's marks the start of another highly inventive period. Were all these projects gestating earlier on?*

It seems to me that all my completed projects not only existed earlier but also forever, except that they emerged with especial seductiveness when their moment came to be considered. It is as though little citadels, little organisms, little nuclei had manufactured themselves while I was busy working elsewhere, and all I had to do was recognize and accept them. All these years I have not felt that I was developing but rather that I was simply running through an already established creative itinerary. And I had to confine myself to pursuing a specific task, to establish its limits, to outline it, in other words to facilitate that whole range of crafts, laboratory and studio, that in my case belong to and fit in with film.

Always, for example, I arrive on the first day of shooting a film without yet having selected all the faces—the people to play the characters. The production unit is in despair; the organizers eye me

199

angrily; but I with superstitious faith nevertheless want to go on. The characters will turn up. It has happened dozens of times and will continue to happen. It even happened in *The Ship Sails On.* Among the other characters I hadn't yet found the night before shooting was a most important one: the princess of an Astro-Hungarian court, blind from birth. Not even I had a good idea of what I was looking for, what I wanted, what face, what actress. I had no real frame of reference with which to select an Astro-Hungarian princess. I never knew one. But lo and behold, in front of me one evening in the confused, sweaty bustle in the loges of the Argentina Theater, amid a flutter of napkins and doors opening and slamming, there was my Austrian princess, timid, composed, diaphanous, dressed in black. She was Pina Bausch. A nun eating ice cream, a saint on roller skates, the face of a queen in exile, of the founder of a religious order, of a judge at a religious tribunal who suddenly winks at you. With her aristocratic face, tender and cruel, mysterious and familiar, constricted in an enigmatic stiffness, Pina Bausch smiled a greeting at me. What a beautiful face. One of those faces destined to transfix us, enormous and disturbing, on the screens of movie houses.

I knew nothing about Pina Bausch. Moreover, I admit my limitations; I have never known much of anything about opera or ballet. I was standing in the orchestra level when I had a sudden urge to go wandering through the corridors to see what was happening behind the scenes or in the empty lobby. I'm ashamed to say it but it bores me to stay until the end. But I watched the scene with Pina Bausch from beginning to end and I would have liked it to go on longer. I felt suddenly seized by a great affection, made a part of such grace, of such a joyous breeze enlivening the scene. And when I wanted to meet her at the end of the show I had new evidence of the good luck that helps me during the preparation of a film. The good luck, as I said earlier, of a journey that spontaneously finds itself on course.

I don't remember any more who said that just as an individual expresses the most secret, mysterious, unexplored part of himself through dreams which reveal his unconscious as well as the collective unconscious, mankind does the same thing in interpreting artistic creations. That is, artistic creation is nothing more than humanity's dream activity. The painter, the poet, the novelist and even the director function by elaborating and organizing with their own talent the content of the collective unconscious and expressing and revealing it on the page, on canvas, or on the screen. It seems to me that if this vision of things is so, then strike any question of limits or restrictions upon artistic activity. Can the unconscious be used up? Can it have limits? Do dreams ever end?

The dream activity of mankind, which seems automatic, becomes an artistic technique, a language of visuals, of symbols. And the artist through his creation perceives a way of setting in order something that already exists, making it flower for the senses and the mind. That is the archetype of creation which renews itself over and over, the journey from chaos to cosmos, from what is jumbled and elusive to order, statement, completeness. Restated: from the unconscious to the conscious. I think that for the artist the feeling of doing is stronger than the achievement itself. It seems to me that anyone working to express something works from within that expression and seeks above all to convey its own reason for being and its own joy. And whatever criticism does away with that condition becomes a dangerous, murky form of self love; through it the critic is led by his own vanity to chat foolishly about what he himself has done and why. Thus he almost always betrays the indefinable phenomenon within himself.

Now to Casanova. *What is the first thing that comes to your mind?*

The alarmed, anxious look of Donald Sutherland which put the fear in me of traps, snares, betrayals.

Everytime I came near him to suggest what he was
to do he stiffened like somebody who scents a
danger he can't escape. I wanted to laugh—those
fears were really comical—but if I laughed it would
make everything even more menacing. If he
thought I was making fun of him his eyes would
fill with tears and his nose, chin, tie clips, wig, and
false eyelashes came undone. Then he looked like
Lionel Atwill in *The Wax Mask* when his face melts
during the fire sequence.

I am convinced that this feminine uneasiness, this
chronic timidity, this incurable shyness
undoubtedly influenced his character, making it
even more strange, distant, ghostlike, just as I
imagined Casanova to be. "But, dear Feffy, why
does your Casanova have to be that way?" The
American producer from Universal Studios asked
me, a big man with a likeable face like Walter
Matthau, who insisted on calling me Feffy and had
two huge hands like cushions with which he
squeezed mine trying to make me see
reason: "Casanova is life! Is life. Is strength,
courage, faith. He is the joy of living. Understand,
Feffy? Why have you made him a zombie?"

Looking at the big face of that fine megabucks
American, who made a pile of films with Gary
Cooper, Clark Gable, Joan Crawford, Huston, Billy
Wilder, who was the intimate of three or four
presidents and who every Saturday was invited over

Casanova: Donald Sutherland

by Nixon to give him advice, I didn't know what to answer. I stammered something about the amniotic sac, Casanova locked in the amniotic sac of a prison-mother, mother-Mediterranean-lagoon-Venice, and of a birth continuously postponed, never achieved: "Casanova—I concluded, blurting it out—was never born. His is a non-life, understand?" A resigned sorrow filled the American's fat face and he shook his head sadly. "Feffy, Feffy, these are mental masturbations, intellectual games!" And then he began telling of the time when he changed the whole ending of a story by Truman Capote, and how "Tru" now considers him a father and doesn't write a line without telephoning him. And when he made Preston Sturges rework a continuity six times. And the memorable day when he told Marlon Brando, "Off with the mustache and lose seven pounds."

I have already said *ad nauseam* that I don't see my films again and therefore am in no position to make an objective detached judgment about them. *Casanova* however seems to me my most complete, expressive, courageous film. You yourself described it as a film version of a horror story. That was the only time I didn't agree with you.

You made Orchestra Rehearsal *for television. Did you do so because of the crisis in filmmaking?*

I have been making films for thirty years, and every year I have heard it said that this was the last, that the cinema was finished, dead, that I would have to go back to scribbling for newspapers, telephone some old publisher or go back to law school to get a doctorate. How long has it been since people stopped going to the movies? And how many times has each of us been invited to diagnose the situation? We have all said: people are afraid to go out at night; the price of tickets; television; the cinema eats its own tail, finds it good and continues eating; permissiveness (the fact that nowadays if you make love in your car some voyeur applauds or some crazy assassin jumps you or your girl, and nothing worse happens to him than a fine and a reprimand); also, the public goes to the movies less often because they go driving, or leave on safari. Now they all go for weekends to the most unreachable places on the planet, so what is the point of showing those "beautiful places" on film when a Saturday morning charter flight gets you there with your whole family?

Someone intelligent has made a more profound analysis, saying that the crisis of the cinema derives especially from the fact that it has exhausted all possible stories, in the classical sense of the word; that nowadays we want something more from the cinema, something that partakes of the scientific, the social, the religious, the philosophical: in sum, a cinema that is truly a more profound mirror in which we are not only reflected as we are but as we have been, as we will be, and perhaps, who knows, as we should have been. I would certainly like to see what a producer looks like who is capable of listening with interest to a film project proposed in those terms.

However I too think that the cinema has lost authority, prestige, mystery, magic. The giant screen that dominates an audience devotedly gathered in front of it no longer fascinates us. Once it dominated tiny little men staring enchanted at immense faces, lips, eyes, living and breathing in another unreachable dimension, fantastic and at the same time real, like a dream. Now we have learned to dominate it. We are bigger than it. See how we have reduced it: here it is the size of a cushion between the library and the flower pot. Sometimes it's even in the kitchen, near the refrigerator. It has become an electric domestic servant and we, seated in armchairs, armed with remote control, exercise a total power over those little images, rejecting whatever is unfamiliar or boring to us.

In a movie house even if we don't like the film the intimidation and fascination of that huge screen makes us stay seated until the end; because of economic togetherness, if for no other reason, having paid for a ticket. But now, with a kind of spiteful revenge, as soon as what we are looking at demands more attention than we wish to pay it, tac! a push with the thumb and we cut off whoever is speaking. We wipe out the images that don't interest us. We are the masters. What a bore that Bergman! Who said Buñuel was a great director? Out of the house with them. I want to see a ball game or a variety show. Thus a tyrant spectator is born, an absolute despot who does what he wants and is more and more convinced that he is the director or at least the producer of the images he sees. How could the cinema possibly try to attract that kind of audience. American producers and directors try to capture the attention of their detached, indifferent, defiant audience by putting on huge spectacles, staggering adventures, galactic catastrophies, magic, horrors, the unforeseeable, the never-before-seen, the unheard of: in sum, a return to the beginning, to the cinema of Méliès, to marvels.

In these great American spectacles I find a tendency to favor ornamentation, scene design, a pyrotechnical cluster of sensational effects working to the detriment not only of a feel for the story but also at times of the story itself. It is a cinema in which the author disappears, a cinema of engineers; they are the ones who merit the applause, the special effects technicians. The ideal would be, as was the case in Kubrick's *2001, Space Odyssey*, that this extraordinary technical equipment be at the service of an idea, a feeling, an author's imagination. When this happens the result will be "marvelous"—to be marveled at—and the cinema will be restored to a realm of total spectacle resem- bling no other art: not theater, not literature, not music, not painting, but rather all of those artistic expressions fused together.

Is it possible to create a cinema like that here in Italy? Not likely. The author who wants to create that kind of cinema absolutely must have an exceptional, irreplaceable, vital collaborator who is . . . the bank. And bankers who sincerely worry about our crisis in the cinema—at least who choose to, are inclined to—don't seem to me to be that numerous. But here I have moved into an area where I function badly, am uninformed. I know that our friends the producers are calling for a law to protect our cinema and not let it choke to death. When they patiently explain to me how such laws can be passed, it seems they are right. However, protective intervention by the State gives me a sense of shame, immediately conjures up mediocrity in ambush, with the cheater and the faker apt to enjoy the same advantages.

Work for television? That means entering that ocean of blurred, confused images, into a hodgepodge that cancels itself out, a substitute for reality quantitatively as well as qualitatively. I have the unpleasant feeling of participating in a catastrophic flood of images, which television subjects us to every minute of the day and night. It wipes out more and more every shred of separation between the real and the visual and substitutes a kind of unreality to which our way of viewing had better get used to: two mirrors facing one another, duplicating themselves with infinite monotony and emptiness. It is not a question of style or of aesthetics. I don't even know what language to use for a television film.

I made *Orchestra Rehearsal* for TV with the one great advantage of flexibility: a production machine more supple, easier, less laborious to run, less burdened with useless ballast, less elephantine. With it I felt less burdened by responsibility and was therefore able to see the project through with greater freshness and spontaneity. Apart from that I haven't done anything different than usual. That is, within my limits and with the few lire at my disposal, to tell stories, to follow my natural inclination toward the marvelous, to express as always what seems to me a disturbing or mysterious or fascinating vision of life.

In sum, although it may seem paradoxical to you, or ridiculous or impertinent or provocative, it seems to me that the only course for our cinema to follow is to make films, better films, more intelligent films, better made films, more beautiful films. Or else we're going to have to resign ourselves to the fact that from now on the cinema will belong to the archivists to store along with many other examples of this century's periods. Soon we'll say that even as the nineteenth century was the century of melodrama, the twentieth has been the century of the cinema.

Orchestra Rehearsal *provoked the most varied reactions. What do you remember about them?*

If I had to try to define the public response, direct and through hearsay, I honestly couldn't begin to classify my film, and maybe that inability is healthy, especially as an example for others. How indeed to reconcile the feelings of those who commented regretfully after the film: "What a shame it didn't finish when the orchestra began playing as a unit again! But why did he suddenly put in German dialogue? What's the point? What does it mean?" How to reconcile all that with the demented manner of that lunatic (because I think he must be quite crazy to interpret the film that way) who, in the cloak room of a restaurant while I was putting on my coat, whispered to me with savage satisfaction: "I've seen the film. I'm on your side. We do need Uncle Adolph here!"

Anxious question: is it ever possible that a film lends itself to so monstrous an error? Or better, what can it mean? What can stimulate or reveal so far out a reaction? Today's world, with its organizational structure crumbling, its values and guideposts nullified, finds each of us reacting to the confusion, sickness, and evil that surrounds us. We generalize our own personal pathology and project our own fears and desires onto everything around us, be it a film or an event.

Perhaps that's the way it had to be from the moment that film showed an insane situation, a downfall into the irrational; since that situation was terrifying we reacted by proposing a form of organized institutionalized insanity, just like in a dictatorship. And thus it comes full circle: if politics pays no attention to us, we pay attention to the politics which condition us totally: he who wants protection must resign himself to being protected to the utmost limits.

City of Women *also addressed quite a modern theme. Searching your memory, what is the first image that emerges?*

Marcello [Mastroianni]. Dear wonderful Marcello. Faithful devoted wise friend, the kind of friend found only in stories by British authors. Marcello and I rarely see one another, almost never.

Perhaps that is one of the reasons for our friendship, a friendship that doesn't pretend, doesn't obligate, doesn't make conditions, doesn't establish rules and boundaries. A truly beautiful friendship, based on a healthy mistrust of one another.

Working with Marcello is a joy: tactful, easy, intelligent, he steps right into the character without ever asking questions, without even having read the scenario. "What fun is there—he says—in knowing in advance what will happen? I prefer to discover it day by day, even as it's happening to the character." He allows himself to be made up, dressed, coiffed without objection, asking for only absolutely indispensable things. With him everything is calm, serene, relaxed, natural, the kind of naturalness that sometimes allows him to sleep during sequences when he is on stage, even in the foreground.

Will I make other films with old "Snaporaz?" I sincerely hope so. The evening I was talking to him about *City of Women* still without telling him he would be the main character—the producer on the other hand was insisting at that time on Dustin Hoffman, and I must say I liked the American actor for the part, considered it a very stimulating choice—Marcello was listening as though hardly interested, like someone who knows the affair doesn't concern him but is obligated through

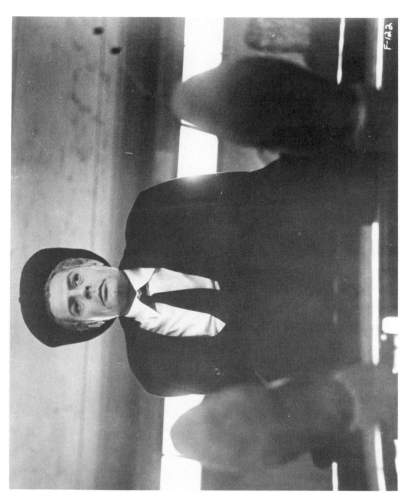

Marcello Mastroianni

friendship and courtesy to display lukewarm curiosity. "It is a story—I said—of a man who studies Woman thoroughly, considers all aspects of her and is fascinated yet dumbfounded by her. He seems to be looking at her without any desire to understand her, rather for the pleasure of remaining dumbfounded, admiring, enraptured, confused and somewhat loving. He is someone in search of a woman, of Woman, but not wanting ever to find her. Perhaps he is afraid; perhaps he thinks that finding Woman and possessing her means to succumb, to disappear, to die. Therefore he prefers to continue searching for her without ever attaining her."

Narrating the film that movingly disturbed me a little. I continued driving the car in silence. Marcello too was quiet. We avoided looking at one another for a length of time. But at that moment, almost unknown to us, it had been decided that we would work together on *City of Women*.

We come to your latest film. Those who worked on the shooting affirm that everything went easily and well, without the tensions and obstacles of other times. The schedules were adhered to with an almost Germanic discipline. Does the credit go to the production, a happy time in your life, or something else?

The Ship Sails On is now behind me and I remember very little about the work on it. To tell the truth I remember fewer and fewer things that happen to me. From the various films I have made only useless and incomprehensible details remain: a machinist's green sweater; exterior sequences with the rain beating against the plastic tent we improvised, huddled together there in a trench in the dark. I have to make a painful effort, and as far as I'm concerned a useless one, to recall the atmosphere of one of my films, which essentially never changes. Perhaps that is why it seems incredible to me that I am sixty-four years old, since I have just stayed inside a studio turning a projector on and off, shouting through a megaphone, and asking for a box lunch at break time.

I don't think the work on *The Ship Sails On* went along any easier than it did on the other films. Maybe it seemed so to the others simply because the filming exactly matched, and was even less than, the number of weeks the work schedule planned for.

Ideal conditions for making a film do not exist; or better still the conditions are always ideal, since they are the ones that allow you to make the film the way you ultimately make it. Our profession combines rigor and elasticity. We have to be firm but also yielding, ready to put up with resistance, disagreements, even mistakes in a spirit of watchful authority. The unforeseen is not always a problem; it is oftentimes a help. Everything is a part of the work on a film, everything is the film.

Tonino Guerra and I wrote *The Ship Sails On* some time ago—as I have already said elsewhere—because I had to express an idea, but I no longer remember to whom. After two or three days of vague chatter and idle reflection we got the plot and continuity ready in only three weeks. If three weeks doesn't seem enough to turn out a good scenario, consider the fact that from the first hints of the story to the start of the filming three years went by. And it seems to me that three years are long enough to guarantee the expectation of a not unworthy film.

At the beginning I was to make it with Gaumont, then Vides, then Dino De Laurentiis, then Aldo Nemni, the Milanese industrialist in love with cinema...finally it was R.A.I. which managed to get everyone (except De Laurentiis) to agree, entrusting the production to Franco Cristaldi.

As has happened to me regularly for fifteen years, living too long with a film project ends up making me hate it. I try to get rid of it; I don't want to work on it any more. And that's the time when the film really gets done.

Now that *The Ship Sails On* is finished I can no longer tell you what my original feeling about it was.

Only that the film exists: what I wanted to do with it has dissolved. I remember talking back then of poignantly fascinating characters with the charm of unknown people's photographs. I said I wanted to make a film in the style of the earliest movies, which therefore had to be in black and white, even streaked and with moisture stains, like a vintage holding in a film library. In sum, a fake, and that is what attracted me, because I think an honest film must be that.

I don't know how many of those intentions remained in the film, because during the shooting things turned up providentially the way they always do. Maybe this time I devoted a little more care than usual to selecting the faces. I believed I needed faces that literally seemed to be those of people who no longer exist: people lost in time who touch us and arouse our curiosity because of that out of date coiffure, that hundred year old garment, that way of smiling, of fixing us with a glance forever lost which reveals a sense of history, the story of a life. I thought that maybe actors from another country, from another society, with different manners and customs could better express that kind of remoteness, that moving alien quality. I think that is the real reason why, besides many Italian actors in this film, there are English, French, and German actors who seem more real because they interpret characters belonging to their own nationalities.

Surrounded by photographs of their faces hung on the walls of my little office at Cinecittà, I felt the need to develop their stories further, to dig more deeply into their relationships, to add friends, parents, new acquaintances, to invent new situations: in sum, to also make the voyage with them. For the film is the story of a voyage, a sea voyage to complete a ritual, a voyage which is supposed to have taken place seventy years ago on the eve of the outburst of the First World War.

Still on The Ship Sails On: *you shot it in color but then you reversed it so that we see certain parts in black and white. Is there some connection here with* 8½, *where "reality" was in black and white and the dream in color?*

The film tells of a far off world which lived and suffered when none of us existed. I wanted the characters of the story to convey the same feeling as when you look at an old photograph. It doesn't matter that such turn of the century photographs would be yellowed and ghostlike, with the sepia tones of a daguerrotype. I think that even if they were stylish and colorful our feelings would intervene and discolor them, make them ghostlike, because for us people like those are shadows. That is why the photography of *The Ship Sails On* has

The Ship Sails On: Freddie Jones

The Ship Sails On: Pina Bausch

an unusual color key: the reds, blues, greens lose the force of reality in order to take on the vague shapes and blurred tones of memory. As in all voyages through time or invasions into the recesses of the past, the reality attained and evoked always has the feel of a relic. It is a document rescued from the depths, from the dust of an archaeological dig, from the sand enveloping it at the bottom of the sea. Its images become somehow distorted, veiled, trembling; there is always something between us and those images. That veil, that distance, I have always wanted to preserve on the screen to suggest the spilling out process which occurs in our minds with the passing years—a process by which reminiscences fittingly appear as evanescent, fluctuating.

That process has nothing in common with the rotten color in *8½* which—perhaps it's not well known—was stupidly decided by the production unit against my will, with the simple minded idea of making it easier for the audience to understand the film by distinguishing dreams from reality.

In general what problems do you find in the tasks following the filming?

What fun would there be in working without problems? Each phase of film work presents unforeseen difficulties; it is part of the job to overcome them or else try to live with them. For me dubbing is one of the most demanding phases. I have to rewrite all the dialogue completely, because my way of making a film prohibits my using even one meter of the original soundtrack. That's a Tower of Babel: voices of every nationality, dialects, prayers, voices which recite numbers instead of giving cues, voices which at my suggestion tell what they had eaten the night before. Dubbing is like remaking the film, this time according to the needs of the soundtrack, which sometimes presents verbal problems as important as the visual ones.

Another delicate phase is montage. During the actual shooting I don't at all mind visits from friends, acquaintances or, as is now the custom, entire classes of students noisily entering the theater. (Their comments don't bother me and I even feel stimulated playing at mountebank or juggler.) However, in the little montage studio I tolerate no presence, except of course the editor and his assistants. I must be alone. This is the phase in which the film begins to reveal itself for what it is. It is like when Dr. Frankenstein, his monster constructed of diverse anatomical parts, makes the stretcher rise up to the storm-filled sky to receive life from the thunderous discharge of the lightning. It is with montage that the film begins to breathe, to move, to look you in the eye.

*Before sending your film to the Venice Film Festival
were you able to review it several times? Have you
corrected, retouched, refined it in every detail or, as often
happens, was the film snatched out of your hand to meet
the deadline?*

It is to be hoped—as I have often had occasion
to say—that once a film is definitely completed I
can let at least a month go by without seeing it,
without thinking about it, without talking about it
any more so that I can review it more serenely and
less constrained by haste. But that will never
happen. With *The Ship Sails On* things went as
always. After the montage I had a first showing with
a soundtrack consisting of my voice, my shouts,
my suggestions. The copy was labeled "work copy"
which, believe me, is always the most beautiful
because it is still confused, dirty, marked up. That
way you look at your film under the illusion that
afterward it will become more alluring, more
fascinating. Instead this rarely happens.

Usually for this kind of showing the lights are
dimmed and the sound regulated. I leave the two
or three friends I've invited (the same ones always,
because I trust them and know that no matter what,
they'll tell me they liked it) and go nosing about
in the booth, chatting a couple of times with the
projectionist, casting a few glances through the glass
to spy, as if by accident, my film down there far

far away on the screen, which begins to perform its seductive task. Or else while the showing continues I go out and sit on the steps of the Cinecittà projection room, sniffed at from a distance by a pack of dogs that by night take over the studio.

One friend tells me he found my film "terrible." We understand one another; he is not referring to its quality but instead means he was most impressed by it. An author, delighted by the happy thought that he has seen something terrifying, feels the film is important. In this case however I don't agree with my friend. If I can hazard a commentary on *The Ship Sails On*, the film seems joyous to me. It seems like a film that makes you want to do another right away.

You have always shown an aversion to world film festivals. Yet you attend the Venice Festival. Don't tell me that you have to go!

Let's be honest. Everyone—as you already know—wants to attend festivals, even those colleagues who in the past bad-mouthed Venice irresponsibly, then ran off to Cannes in top hat and tails.

There is some risk in going, it's true, but that's the same in every arena where competition takes place. In the end, even not to participate is a risk. On the other hand when the producer is happy, the distributor too, and the actresses and actors absolutely beaming, why be a spoil sport? And the festival directors go out of their way to assure you you don't run any risk, since you're out of the competition. It seems that when you reach a certain age it is more distinguished to present your film outside the competition. And my grumblings, which imply that instead I would be willing to compete, because that seems even more distinguished to me, are taken as wisecracks.

The truth is that if they guaranteed me the prize I would most willingly compete. And speaking of the prize: don't they always say that the festivals encourage and favor a film which, in intent at least, does not resort to box office spectacle? Then why not finally decide to give cash prizes? The first festival to introduce the custom of awarding an impressive check to the most distinguished films would become the most important in the world.

I have made about twenty films and this is the twentieth time I have been invited to the festival. The experience should have made me a little skeptical and rather relaxed. Instead I must confess that it is still exciting and even a little disturbing: the arrival at the Lido by motorboat or at the Croisette in an air conditioned Mercedes; the flags from all over the world fluttering on the palaces where the films are shown; the frenzied or relaxed comings and goings; the nervous and sweaty employees in the halls of the great hotels; meeting the inevitable producer with the exotic accent, dressed all in white except for his olive green face, who invites you to make a film at El Badush because El Badush seems made just for you; the press conferences. . .

Ah, yes. . .press conferences. You don't seem to like them much. But aren't they a part of your profession?
Finding myself blocked behind a table at two in the afternoon in August with three or four microphones under my nose—I have already said this before—explaining why there's a rhinocerous in my film is not exactly my favorite situation. I feel almost total discomfort chatting about what I have done. I get the uncomfortable feeling I have to defend myself, now or never, by embellishing my film, painting and powdering it with words, inventing justifications in a desperate effort to give it profundity of thought, visual originality. I take that all too seriously; I don't manage to be objective; I'm not sprightly: in sum, I'm ill.

Sometimes I've tried to avoid press conferences, but my action seemed arrogant and impolite—even some friends were offended. Actually it was only timidity, a sense of proportion and a desire not to be boring. If I say there's a rhinocerous in my film because maritime specialists assured me that in 1914 every ship had to carry one in its hold, friends of the press think, and justly so, that I am trying with poor success to make a joke. If I say instead that in the belly of the ship, in its depths, the Id resides, our unconscious, our animal part which transcending time and space nevertheless sustains our existence, forcing us necessarily and providentially to co-exist with it, I see that everyone is happier with such a response—but I feel a little ridiculous . . .

I would like a silent press conference where we would look at one another, smile at one another, wave at one another, even exchange gifts all without saying a word, and then everyone would go about his business.

Seeing your film again in Venice, did you have a different feeling from what you expected?

On this point too I will repeat things already said. It is a cruel custom which makes a writer attend the chewing, swallowing, gulping down of his own film into the stomach of an immense movie house. Your film on the screen has its own pulsebeat and you observe that the audience has a different one, two hearts out of phase beating arhythmically. This duality, this lack of synchronicity cuts through you, unsettles you, makes you ill, tortures you.

And how to rescue yourself from this torture, when, what's more, you're seated near a minister, a beautiful woman, the Grand Duke and cannot slip away? I close my eyes and begin to remember past events, pleasant encounters, luscious adventures; I also make calculations like how many times a year I did a certain thing; I imagine answering letters promptly that I have in my pocket: in sum, I escape in every way possible from the showing of the film which runs on relentlessly and never ends.

From time to time I open one eye and look at my film, which makes me a little sad, abandoned as it is to its destiny in front of thousands of eyes seeing who knows what. Even to my own eyes my films sometimes look different. It depends on the city in which I see them, the movie house, the people whom I'm with. Films are unstable, changing, moody, according to the times and the seasons in which they are shown. They mirror the moods of the movie house. Is the movie house boring? The film too becomes more boring. The public doesn't understand the film? Then it becomes more unfathomable than ever. That's why I don't ever want to see my films again, or perhaps only in the most advanced old age when, having completely forgotten them, they can appear to me as they really are for the first time.

*Old age again: do we want to conclude this interview
the way it began? Fellini at eighty, Fellini at ninety.
How do you see yourself? What is your future schedule?*

Memory. It's failing. I have trouble remembering
the names of people and also certain words at times.
Many years ago I thought that during my old age
I would read the books that have faithfully waited
for me, that I would wander around museums I
have never visited: India, Tibet. I have a friend
in Benares; we write to one another often. One time
he told me that with the power of his mind he
managed to materialize my alter ego in his garden.
That feat eliminated my desire to go and visit him.

I comfort myself by thinking of the great old men
whom Simone de Beauvoir speaks of in her
beautiful book. I have read and reread the pages
devoted to Tolstoy, Verdi, Victor Hugo. I hoped
to find some analogies there. Nothing.

I read somewhere that D'Annunzio, when quite
advanced in years, was taken one evening to a
performance of one of his tragedies. The play was
in his honor and all officialdom was there as well
as high society. D'Annunzio, seated in the first row,
did nothing but laugh. He interrupted the actors,
insulted them, wanted to know who was the author
of that piece of crap and flayed him up and down.
And the more the faces around him lengthened with
dismay the more the poet, completely gone,
exploded with laughter.

Final question: what is left for you to say in a coming film?

I don't know. After so many death knells, after getting so much pleasure out of ruins and decay, I would like to make those people happy—women for the most part—who, with a gently frustrated manner and a hopeful anticipation in their voices have repeated after each of my films: "But why don't you ever make a beautiful love story?"